TEACHING
CHRISTIANITY

TEACHING
CHRISTIANITY

W. Owen Cole and Ruth Martin

Heinemann Educational Publishers
Halley Court, Jordan Hill, Oxford OX2 8EJ

MADRID ATHENS PARIS
FLORENCE PRAGUE WARSAW
PORTSMOUTH NH CHICAGO SAO PAULO
SINGAPORE TOKYO MELBOURNE AUCKLAND
IBADAN GABORONE JOHANNESBURG

First published 1994

98 97 96 95 94
10 9 8 7 6 5 4 3 2 1

British Library Cataloguing in Publication Data
A catalogue record for this book is available from the British Library

ISBN 0 435 30150 0

Typeset by TechType, Abingdon, Oxon
Printed and bound in Great Britain by Clays Ltd, St Ives plc

Acknowledgements

The authors and publishers would like to thank the following for their permission to reproduce copyright material:
The Bible Societies/HarperCollins Publishers Ltd for the extracts from the *Revised Standard Version Common Bible*, 1973, on pp. 60–3, 65, 76, 107–8, 125; SCM Press for the extract from *How to Read the New Testament* by Etienne Charpentier on p. 71 and for the extract from *The Quest for the Historical Israel* by George W Ramsey on p. 34.

The authors would also like to thank Paul Baker, Douglas Charing and the many colleagues, friends and students who have helped knowingly or unwittingly. Sue Walton, Alistair Christie and other members of Heinemann's staff have given us valuable advice and assistance.

Finally, our own families have exercised the patience, and provided the encouragement, without which this book could never have been written. Our special thanks go to Peter, Gwynneth, Michael and Naomi.

Owen Cole and Ruth Mantin

Contents

Introduction

RELIGIOUS EDUCATION was made legally compulsory in 1944 and that position was reaffirmed in 1988, together with the explicit statement that it should be taught to all those registered as full time pupils in a school. This cleared up any doubts about its place in the curriculum of sixth formers; it must be part of their education (Circular 1/94, paragraphs 5 and 11, pages 9 and 10). It remains, however, the least taught subject and the Cinderella of the curriculum, with respect to time and money allocation and the provision of professionally qualified staff, even though the government stresses its importance (Circular 1/94 paragraphs 1 to 14, pages 9 to 11). (It should be noted that we often refer to the 1988 Act rather than that of 1993. This is because the 1993 Act tends to endorse rather than change the 1988 provisions. It is the Department for Education Circular 1/94 which really updates regulations relating to the actual teaching of Religious Education.)

We acknowledge that the teaching of Christianity is often neglected in favour of topics relating to being kind and good, which are usually forms of moralizing. Religionless topics, rather than cross-religion approaches, seem to be the reality and the problem. There are understandable reasons for this which we try to address in the first part of our book. Until they are faced and dealt with, Religious Education, and especially Christianity, will not be adequately taught.

Our aim is to persuade teachers that Christianity can be taught and that all professional teachers of good will are capable of teaching it. The context of such teaching must be that of an awareness of the world's plurality of faiths, brought into our homes daily by the media. (You might take a week at random to check this, not neglecting adverts, which sometimes have a religious connection. It could be a mini-research project for Key Stage 3 or Key Stage 4 pupils.

Even if the 1988 Act did not require us to 'take account of the teachings and practices of the other principal religions represented in Great Britain', as well as recognizing that Christianity is the main tradition, (chapter 40, part 1, section 8), it would be difficult to ignore them. DfE Circular 1/94 also states that an Agreed Syllabus, the legal Local Education Authority document which prescribes what should be taught in Religious Education, 'should not be designed to convert pupils, or to urge a particular religion or religious belief on pupils' (paragraph 32, page 15). That cannot be done convincingly if children are taught only about one religion, whichever it might be. Whether the legal requirement to hold a daily act of collective worship is compatible with an open approach to Religious Education lies beyond the scope of this book, but we must admit that it has caused us difficulties.

This book is specifically about Christianity, but we are commited to the view that it must be taught in a world religions context. We would draw attention to the danger of teaching Christianity in such a way that a child may go home to a non-religious parent and say: 'You're not good, Mummy. My teacher says all good people believe in Jesus'. It is also very easy to convey the idea that only Christians care, if the only exemplars which children learn about are Christian (probably white, usually male and often dead – which says something about Christianity as a living faith!).

Alternatively, if Christianity is taught alongside other world religions, it all too often seems to suffer by comparison because of the methods used. Children engage in all sorts of exciting activities when they study these, but the traditional approach to Christianity presents it as dull, lifeless and boring. We believe that Christianity is as fascinating, colourful, diverse and enjoyable to teach and study as any other religion. Teaching Christianity, however, requires particular sensitivity and training because of the place of the religion in British society.

We hope that by the time you reach the end of the book (though there is no need for you to work through Part 2 in chapter order), you will feel able to teach Christianity with some confidence. However, there is a need for more than the support that we can give. Schools need to treat Religious Education fairly by giving it at least 5 per cent of timetable time and 5 per cent of financial resources, remembering in doing so that it does not cease to be taught at Key Stage 4, like some other subjects, and ensuring that in primary schools there is a co-ordinator for Religious Education who has some professional qualification in the subject. In secondary schools Religious Education should have parity with, say, History in every possible way, ranging from the opportunity for Religious Studies to be taken at GCSE and A level to its being taught by adequately qualified and professionally trained graduates. LEAs and the Government have their part to play, too. We write at a time when LEA advisers and inspectors and advisory teachers are disappearing swiftly, and we write from within an authority which appointed its first inspector six years ago and has witnessed a positive transformation in Religious Education as a result. Unless those who possess power guarantee the delivery of Religious Education by giving practical backing, the future will be as dismal as the past has often been.

Non-specialist students are fortunate if they receive a 15-hour course in Religious Education as part of their initial teacher training and INSET provision for those who find themselves anxiously attempting to teach the subject is rare. OFSTED is probing primary schools where it has never actually appeared in the curriculum. Instead of damning reports, which demoralize teachers, short, government-backed INSET courses should be spread over the next five years. Otherwise the School Curriculum and Assessment Authority's Model Syllabuses will create panic, and might lead to the undesirable consequence of teachers withdrawing from teaching Religious Education rather than face another daunting challenge.

Finally, parents cannot escape our attention. We look to them to tell their children that the study of beliefs and values is important. All too frequently we find parents saying apologetically: 'Jim won't be doing RE for GCSE. He wanted to, but we told him it won't help him to get a job!' Of course, if children heed that advice there will be no future for Religious Education because there will be no one qualified to teach it.

Many church members cannot distinguish between the role of church and non-denominational schools in matters relating to Religious Education. Some church leaders seem equally confused. They think that the purpose of RE is to produce Christians. No wonder many teachers conclude that they cannot teach Christianity, for only a minority of them, especially in our primary schools, are Christians. In fact, most Christians who are engaged in teaching Religious Education recognize that it would be improper to try to nurture or convert pupils, even if it were possible. Circular 1/94 is perfectly clear on this point, as we have already seen. (Every school should possess a copy of DfE Circular 1/94, *Religious Education and Collective Worship*.) This rejection of proselytizing underlies its statement of the aim of Religious Education:

'Religious Education in schools should seek: to develop pupils' knowledge, understanding and awareness of Christianity, as the predominant religion in Great Britain, and the other principal religions represented in the country; to encourage respect for those holding different beliefs; and to help promote pupils' spiritual, moral, cultural and mental development.'
(Paragraph 16, page 12)

Such aims are clearly incompatible with attempts to replace the beliefs which children bring to school with another set of beliefs, or with ignoring them.

The teacher's role is that of enabling a conversation, a dialogue, or even an argument to take place between beliefs, values and practices and the pupil. For this we must know our children, understand approaches to Religious Education and know enough about the religion to help the conversation to begin. We hope that we have done this in respect of Christianity. Other books provide similar assistance to understanding and teaching about other religions.

You may be able to persuade parents and governors to read this book, or at least the first part of it, to recognize that Religious Education is worthwhile and demanding, and an essential curriculum area which they should encourage practically. Whether you do or not, we hope that you will find the book helpful and discover that teaching Christianity in a world religions context can be enjoyable. We hope that children studying it will learn that it can be fun.

Ruth Mantin and W Owen Cole,
Chichester, Easter 1994

PART 1

1 Why we haven't taught Christianity and why we should

The RE heritage

We have never taught Christianity. That might come as a shock to some readers but it is true. Bear with us while we explain.

A cursory glance at the Bristol Agreed Syllabus of 1960, entitled *Syllabus of Christian Education*, and those which went before it, should be enough to convince us that the content of RE was mostly biblical and historical. In the sixth form, doctrine and a desire to show that Christianity had nothing to fear from science, scientific Humanism or other religions dominated the Syllabus. There was a section called 'How Christians worship', which could be taught in Years 9 and 10, but the approach was to examine the question 'how' in an ecumenical way, rather than analyze the purpose of worship. It was assumed by most of those who taught RE that knowledge of biblical and historical facts and an introduction to Christian beliefs at the appropriate stage was all that was necessary. Children went to church and/or Sunday school. They knew what worship meant. We were nurturers, helping children to grow into the Christian faith. Few children would admit to not going to church and it was rare to find teachers who expressed any unease about engaging in the nurturing process. Those who withdrew from RE or school worship were usually Roman Catholics and Jews. Most other primary school teachers went through the motions of at least telling a Bible story. The situation of massive evasion of RE which exists at present seems to have been rare.

The present confusion

RE should certainly be about the here and now, but we are the products of our past; and in RE we may be prisoners of it. For example, we often come across students who studied Christianity as an option at GCSE or A level, but who never made the kind of educational visit to a church that they did to a mosque or a synagogue. Presumably it was assumed that there was no need. Perhaps you would like to find out what the Key Stage 2, 3 or 4 children you teach actually know about the inside of a church, what happens there, and, at Key Stage 3 certainly, why.

David Pascall, when he was chairman of the National Curriculum Council, suggested that:

'...two-thirds of our primary school children receive little or no observable RE...and an alarming number of children could be receiving something like 50 hours of RE in their whole school life.'

(Speech to Association of RE Advisers and Inspectors, 1992)

We know from our own experiences, and those of students who return from teaching practice, that a major reason for this situation is the belief of many teachers that RE has not changed since they were primary school children in the '60s and much of the '70s. (Often they are correct.) They imagine that our first paragraph describes RE as it is now. Not surprisingly, they cannot teach it, and secondary head teachers who share this view refuse to invest money or appoint qualified teachers when they think that all you need is faith, and probably love as well! (The requirement for a daily act of worship seems to endorse their view and may be more effective in putting this group of teachers off RE than all that we have written in this book and elsewhere.) It must be remembered that especially in secondary schools, the public face of RE for 95 per cent of teachers is what they see in the hall. They imagine that what happens is a continuation of this.

There are those who would like the Bristol Agreed Syllabus of 1960 to be the pattern for the '90s. Some want it because they would like to recreate Britain as a Christian country. They would proselytize even though the Circular 1/94 guidelines for teaching RE forbid it. Others are motivated by the wish to return to traditional values, those of the period prior to World War II at least, which inspired our resistance to the racial and religious intolerance of Hitler. These people are seldom professionals in the field of education and are never teachers of RE. Their pressure as parents, governors or politicians goes a long way to convincing teachers that Bristol 1960 is alive and well. They must bear considerable responsibility for the frequent lack of support for RE in school staff rooms.

The reality of the '90s is that perhaps fewer than 20 per cent of teachers and children are Christian in any meaningful sense, however one cares to try to assess it. Even though teachers are probably among the more conservative members of society in matters of values, they are more a cross-section of it than in the days when most primary school teachers attended denominational training colleges and almost all were expected to provide a reference from a clergyman when seeking to become a student or, later, a teacher.

The Christian outlook on life is no longer part of the British heritage, picked up through the traditional avenues of parental belief or the media. In the 1992 election, perhaps for the first time ever, a significant number of people explicitly, on TV, challenged the view that it was the responsibility of the better-off to help the weaker members of society – a basic so-called Christian virtue.

The reality regarding courses, of whatever kind, leading to Qualified Teacher Status is that the 30 or 40 hours' preparation for RE, which students intending to teach in primary schools usually received up to about 1970, has now been whittled away to no more than 10 or, at best, 15 hours, as Mathematics and language work, and now the rest of the National Curriculum, compete for time. This gives little enough time to help students understand the purpose of RE today, and to acquire a few of the skills needed to teach RE to children from a society which is sceptical, indifferent and often hostile to religion; none to teach them about any religions. In the days of curriculum inertia it was possible to be sure that the primary teaching which students had received stood them in good stead for their return to the primary classroom as teachers, even if it prepared them for no other occupation. Now they can no longer fall back on that reservoir of knowledge. Even if they could, it would only lead them to disaster. Society has changed; the outlooks of earlier days have gone in RE, as in everything else.

The consequence for teaching about Christianity in this situation is that it must be taught in the way which has long been applied to educating children about Islam or Buddhism in our schools: that is, without any assumptions of prior knowledge or belief. We have to teach about the beliefs, practices and values of Christians but, more than this, we have to keep in mind the world view or outlook of Christians.

The Christian world view is discussed in Chapter 4. We introduce it at this point to stress the importance of understanding the way men and women see the world before it is possible to appreciate most areas of knowledge. The lavish expenditure of some people on clothes or fine cars, while depriving themselves and their families of good food; the journeys from Devon which are made some 50 times a season by a soccer fan to see her favourite team, Manchester United; dining at the Ritz; the frugality of an ascetic; the pilgrimage to Lourdes or Makkah; keeping kosher – all of these are meaningless activities until we understand how the people who undertake them view the world. 'I can't understand why most Germans followed Hitler' is still an oft-heard comment. Understanding is possible if the questioner is willing to work hard to achieve an analysis of the world as Germans saw it in the late 1920s and '30s. Often 'can't understand' is the only phrase children can use. It challenges us to realize that spending £2,000 on the pilgrimge to Makkah or £6 million on Salisbury Cathedral is meaningless to the outsider. In RE we should always consider the child, as well as the teacher, to be an outsider. When we teach about the beliefs, practices or values of a religion we must at least be aware of the outlook on life from which they take their meaning. By the time pupils leave school they should understand what it means to be a Christian in terms of world view, beliefs, values and practices.

Why teach Christianity?

There are several answers to this question. The acceptable one depends on our view of RE. Here are some.

To make children Christians

That might be acceptable in denominational schools, but as long ago as the Church of England Durham report on Religious Education of 1970, it was stated that:
'to press for the acceptance of a particular faith or belief system is the duty and privilege of the Churches and similar bodies. It is certainly not the task of the teacher in a county school.'
(Paragraph 217)

The paragraph continues:
'If the teacher is to press for any conversion, it is conversion from a shallow and unreflective attitude to life.'

As we have already seen, rejection of conversion as an aim is one which has not yet been accepted by everyone, despite the Government itself stating as recently as 1994 that Agreed Syllabuses should:
'...not be designed to convert children or urge a particular religion or religious belief on children.'
(Circular 1/94, paragraph 32, page 15)

Those who wish to use RE for this purpose are breaking the law.

To make children moral

The government white paper *Choice and Diversity*, which underlay the 1993 Education Act, and many pronouncements since, have stressed the importance of children knowing 'right from wrong'. We accept that it is important for children to be morally aware and educated in such a way that they can make moral choices. RE has a part to play in this process. The National Curriculum Council discussion paper *Spiritual and Moral Development* (April 1993) attached great importance to Religious Education and to Collective Worship (pages 6 and 7). However, it is no use expecting the 'Cinderella subject' suddenly to acquire respect and status. Almost the whole curriculum is potentially value-laden so to confine the exploration of morals to RE is to convey a message which will result in little or no change in the nation's moral outlook. More seriously still, values are the products of belief. Teachers are unlikely to have any success in preaching or teaching Christian morality to pupils who do not accept the world view on which they are based. In a society which is really secular, values cannot be prescribed by religion.

The moral argument for teaching Religious Education cannot be sustained when confronted by reality. We consider it to be improper anyway, except to the extent that History, Geography, Science, and the rest of the curriculum have similar responsibilities for the moral development of children.

To enable children to become fully educated

There would seem to be two valid reasons for teaching Christianity:

1 Religious Studies, or the Study of Beliefs and Values (which is what we would prefer to call it), must include religions as areas of study. Christianity is numerically the largest as well as the most widely distributed religion in the world. It is inconceivable that it should not be included in a programme of Religious Studies. Anyone who does omit it should examine their motives critically

2 there is a need for all children growing up in Britain to understand the religion which has influenced our society so much, just as there would be a need for anyone growing up in Pakistan to understand Islam. If, however, we expect Muslim children in Britain to listen to the story of Christianity, we must also expect non-Muslims to listen to the story of Islam, otherwise Muslims will naturally conclude that their religion is not valued and that the real purpose of RE is conversion.

The only justification for RE must be educational. Children have a right to study and explore the beliefs, values and practices upon which many people base their lives and which underpin many cultures and individual lives just as much as they have a right to learn about humanity's past, literature, music and art, science and languages. The justification for learning about Christianity must be based on a view of education which finds a place for understanding beliefs and values.

Most of the rest of this book is about what of Christianity to teach and suggested approaches, so these issues will not be discussed here. There is, however, a need to consider the ground rules and some basic issues: things that have to be sorted out before we close the classroom door behind us and begin teaching. This is what we turn to in the next chapter.

2 Rules of engagement

In teaching any child any subject and any religion, especially Chrsitianity in Britain, there are certain guidelines to be followed and issues to be considered. The context is that of recognizing the importance of Christianity; teaching it in a way which is respectful of Christianity; and respecting the integrity of the child. This means no proselytizing, which is illegal anyway.

Commitment

This is the first key issue for many teachers and causes them considerable anxiety. Much has been written about this matter, often from the standpoint of the teacher. This is important of course, but let us remember the child, the subject and the purpose of education in a democracy such as Britain, as well. Teachers are, or should be, people who can take care of themselves. They are adults who enjoy an extremely privileged position, being responsible for forming the attitudes of children, as well as helping them to develop their concepts, attitudes and skills. Governments may not rate them highly, but society should. In this context we might ask: what should be a teacher's first commitment? You might like to reflect on this from your own perspective before reading further.

A Muslim, Christian or Humanist could reply that their first responsibility is to their faith. Their reply would be quite proper. Teaching would be a vocation for them, the consequence of their belief. However, how do we expect faith to come across in practice in the classroom? Should it appear as evangelism or as heightened professionalism – and what does that glib phrase mean? We leave you to consider what difference, if any, you would expect to find between a person motivated to become a teacher by a particular belief and one who was doing it for a living. When it comes to teaching RE who should do it better – the believer or the professionally trained teacher? Views on this vary considerably on lines such as the following:

- only the believer can put across the feel of a religion
- a believer is bound to be insensitive to the doubts and views of those who don't share his or her beliefs
- believers stand so close to their beliefs that they cannot be objective
- you have to experience something (like worship) to teach about it.

Each of these arguments has some weight. We have known people who would not accept any belief label, who are excellent teachers of the kind of RE described in this book. We have also come across Christians, Humanists and others who were unable to cope with its demands. Whatever religion one is studying, it is important that, sooner or later, one should meet adherents or, if that is not possible, read material written by them. One should also watch videos or attend acts of worship of the faiths being studied. School worship is no substitute for this. Most participants do not stand within the faith, and the form of school worship, however good it might be, cannot by law possess the characteristics found in a church. Circular 1/94 states:

'...worship in schools will necessarily be of a different character from worship amongst a group with beliefs in common.'

In addition, it says that while worship should 'be wholly or mainly of a broadly Christian character', it 'should not be distinctive of any particular Christian denomination.'

(Paragraph 61 page 21)

Successful RE teaching, within the aims put forward in this book, is primarily a professional exercise. Teachers have to suspend judgement and their own beliefs in order to present sympathetically and accurately the views being examined. Here the situation is not unique. The Jew who lost relatives in the Holocaust has probably a much more difficult problem to cope with if he is to study the history of the Third Reich successfully. Some Jews might not be able to do that; some ex-prisoners of the Japanese might not be able to examine World War II in the Pacific; some Muslims might not be able to help children understand Christian beliefs which are at variance with the Qur'an. Some Christians may have the same kind of difficulty in teaching the Muslim view of Jesus, Jewish concepts of messiahship or, even more important, the Jewish scriptures as something other than the Old Testament.

At the end of the day it is preferable that these people are honest rather than hypocritical, and do not teach things with which they cannot cope even after having made a sincere effort, especially with younger children who may not be able to detect their position. However, anyone who falls into this category should ask: 'How can we expect children to do what we cannot manage? Is it reasonable to ask a Muslim child, for example, to try to understand what Jesus means to Christians if I, as a Christian adult, cannot understand the Muslim view of him?' The logical consequence of this position is the end of education and an admission that we can only understand ourselves! (And how many psychiatrists would endorse that view?)

Here we come to the point of realizing that the child has a background of belief, as well as the teacher. Tenderness of conscience is not something adults should talk about to the neglect of the vulnerable susceptibilities of the children for whom they are responsible. Children have feelings and commitments, too.

Imagine you are a Muslim child and your teacher tells you: 'Now that you are living here, you must learn about our religion', and in every way informs you that what you possess has no worth – your language, the food you eat, the colour of your skin, and your parental faith. Even your name is a problem. Even if one wished to convert the child to Christianity, it is tactically bad to begin by devaluing these things, and a poor witness to Jesus, who respected men and women for what they were. It is not religion but racism and certain political ideologies of an extreme left or right wing nature which devalue the individual in this way.

Finally, classroom evangelism in our maintained schools would seem to be untrue to the precepts of the great religions and an intrusion upon the basic human right to freedom of religion. Many of us would prefer RE not to exist than envisage it being used for sectarian purposes. Those who hold this view are themselves believers, many of them Christians, but others are Baha'is, Buddhists, Hindus, Humanists, Jews, Muslims or Sikhs.

Fortunately, this abandonment of RE is not the only alternative to evangelism. If it were, it would only leave children ignorant and a prey to those unscrupulous groups in all societies which wish to manipulate them for narrow religious or racist purposes. The alternative set out in this book is a form of RE which examines beliefs and values in an open way, which is respectful to the traditions being studied and to the home faith, if they have one, which children bring to school. It is commitment to this kind of RE that teachers should be seeking to promote, in the context of an education which has similar aims. It must, of necessity, be critical, in the best sense of the word. This may be alarming to some believers in all the major faiths, as well as to those politicians who see education as an agent for nurturing children into a culture and predetermined set of values, rather than as a process which is constantly challenging accepted norms and nostrums. Here, RE finds itself caught up in a greater debate, to which it has much to offer, and from which it can disengage only if it is prepared to lose its vitality and worth.

Sometimes we are accused of suggesting through our religious studies approach to RE that all religions are relatively true but that none is the true religion. This is to misunderstand our aim, which is to understand religion in the fullest sense of the word. This includes helping children to appreciate what it means to take a religion seriously; how Christians' or Buddhists' faith affects their whole outlook on life. It should include, at an appropriate place, in the secondary school, an examination of how believers who claim, as all do, that their religion is true respond to the other faiths whose existence they have now to acknowledge, even if they ignored them in the past. This can then be done in the only proper context: one of understanding and knowing about a variety of life stances in an open way, without the desire to assert the supremacy of any, and from a position of respect for each. The primary school has played its part by providing some knowledge and understanding, but even more important respect for the worth of each child, including the beliefs, if any, which they bring from home to the school.

We have paid considerable attention to commitment because it lies at the heart of so many anxieties teachers have. To avoid indoctrination, some Christian teachers avoid teaching Christianity; some agnostics or atheists avoid it too, so as not to convey their prejudices. The result is the teaching of little or no Christianity, so that children are deprived of their right to learn about it.

Instead of avoidance there are some possible reponses. Some teachers favour disclosing their personal commitment. Before accepting that position it might be salutary to ask whether one should also make one's non-commitment public, too. Would parents approve equally of the RE teachers who said: 'I am an atheist/agnostic/Humanist', and the one who said: 'I am a Christian', in answer to the pupil's question? Is the child likely to make value judgements based on our admissions? Children are very impressionable, especially in the primary school, where teachers are often role models.

If a pupil says: 'Miss, what do you believe..?' we would always counsel answering a question with a question: 'Why do you want to know?' and exploring the context as fully as possible. The aim should be to create a 'Let's find out' situation, where children know the purpose of what they are doing. The content of RE should not be confined to the study of the teacher's beliefs and the children's, and we should not place ourselves in the position of having to say, at best: 'No, I don't actually believe...but...'. The 'but' reply is fraught with risks, especially that of being unintentionally patronizing and dismissive – 'No, I'm not, but I respect the religion very highly, of course'.

We would not want to tell pupils what our religious commitment is. We would prefer to focus on the topic being studied, not on our personalities or those of any members of the class. If they wish to disclose where they stand that will be up to them. We would feel that it was our responsibility to enable any child who did volunteer their position to feel reassured and supported by our attitude towards them and their religion or non-religion. They might well express their views very inadequately and perhaps aggressively. We should respond by realizing that it is probably the parents who are actually speaking, and that the child needs to be helped to develop and articulate their own views.

On the subject of commitment, we would say that the commitment we seek is to understanding how people have found and do find meaning in life. Because the subject is RE, most attention, but by no means all, would be given to the understanding of religions. Our commitment is to the study of beliefs, values and religious practices because of their intrinsic importance, and we would certainly let our classes know what our aims are. If pupils then wish to form their own systems of beliefs and values as a consequence of the Religious Education course, that is their right and privilege. It is not our purpose, though the equipment for doing so will have been one of the skills acquired during the period of study.

Listening to the children

Children have their ideas and questions. Teachers are constantly in danger of being didactic, especially in the current educational climate, which seems to place the emphasis on children being 'told' rather than 'finding out'. In a subject like RE, teenagers are likely to switch off if they feel that they are being preached at, and a world religions syllabus can be evangelical, in attempting to persuade students that religion, as opposed to non-religion, is good, even if no particular one is being recommended! Secondary pupils need to feel that they have a share in the syllabus; primary children should at least know that their questions and contributions will be taken seriously. We know of many Sikh, Muslim and other children who wanted to tell their teacher about Guru Nanak's birthday or Eid, only to be ignored, and of Christian children who wanted to share some important event in their religious lives, such as a baptism, harvest festival or confirmation, but the teacher shut them up. Why? Perhaps the teachers felt that they were going to find themselves in deep water, having to talk about things of which they were ignorant. If a climate of shared knowledge, finding out, instead of relying on the teacher-expert, could be created, the teacher might feel less threatened.

Encouraging children to contribute also has its rules. If they do, they should be supported against those who might be inclined to rubbish their beliefs. Hopefully, however, a climate can be created in the classroom in which each is respectful of the other, and one that will persist in the corridor and playground, too. The child who wishes to remain silent should also be respected. One sixth-former, whose father was a vicar, was consulted as the class Christian whenever issues arose – and not only in RE. She considered becoming an atheist, but realized that such a conversion would not save her:

she would then be consulted as the class atheist! The stories other students tell us are often those of personal faith being damaged through being ignored or exposed against their wishes.

There is much discussion about the proportion of time which should be given to Christianity as opposed to other religions, and about how many religions should be studied. Any division into percentages is invidious. We have never been surprised to hear that 'our Muslims aren't interested in RE' when we discover that Islam gets half a term in year 10, the rest being Christianity. In a class which has four religions represented in it, we would find it impossible to decide which two or three should be studied if the Agreed Syllabus is so restrictive. And there is no wisdom in choosing those which are not represented, as an exponent of Buddhism once suggested in a public lecture on multi-faith RE.

Being professional

If we are to respect the integrity of pupil, teacher and the religion being studied, we then have to make sure that we teach in an open, professional way. This means a number of things.

First, our stance must be one of talking about what *Christians* do and believe, not about what *we* believe. It is very easy to say: 'When you go to church', or 'Eid is like our Christmas'. We shouldn't fall into the trap of assuming that there are Christians in the class.

Secondly, comparisons with Christianity should be avoided. Unless a child is a Christian, they are likely to be unhelpful. A remark in a very bad text book that 'The Qur'an is about as long as the New Testament' assumed a knowledge about the New Testament which the reader probably lacked. It also suggested that the norm or reference point is Christianity. Eid is sometimes called the Muslim Christmas but it is not at all like Christmas. There is no Santa Claus, tree, story about the birth of a baby... . The only thing they have in common is celebration. How helpful is it for us to inform you that Hindu upanayam and Sikh amrit pahul have certain points of similarity? The comparisons that we make between another religion and Christianity are often just as confusing to our pupils.

Respect for other religions

Respect for others' beliefs is another context in which we need to teach.

Paragraph 9, page 10 of Circular 1/94 states:
'The Government also attaches great importance to the role of religious

education and collective worship in helping to promote among pupils a clear set of personal values and beliefs. They have a role in promoting respect for and understanding of those with different beliefs and religious practices to their own, based on rigorous study of the different faiths. This country has a long tradition of religious freedom which should be preserved.'

How we teach about the Old Testament, the Pharisees, 'an eye for an eye and a tooth for a tooth' and refer to Judaism generally, along with Hindu polytheism and the Muslim view of Jesus, will be dealt with elsewhere. Here we note that we are legally required to do so in the spirit of the above quotation.

There is a need for the books we use to meet certain criteria. The Other Faiths Committee of the Council of Churches for Britain and Ireland drew up the following guidelines, which teachers might bear in mind when they are looking at inspection copies. We shall refer to books and AVA (audio-visual aids) throughout this book. Meanwhile we must express concern that too many resource materials on Christianity are written from a position of faith on the assumption that the users will be insiders, members of the faith. For this reason they are often inferior to resources for the teaching of other religions and, bearing in mind the paragraph quoted above, they may actually be illegal!

Books on Christianity should:

1 demonstrate that the author has a clear understanding of the overall faith so that the particular topic, e.g. worship, is being examined in the context of a Christian world view. This may be implicit rather than explicit in the book, but without it the reader is likely to be faced only with information which might seem curious. For example, why people should sing hymns only makes sense when the reader appreciates the faith relationship which inspires Christians to do it. The same might be said of the 'silent worship' of Friends. Someone who does not understand their world view might think that they are just sitting around doing nothing

2 be factually accurate

3 be appropriate to the age, aptitude and family background of pupils. We would not expect material on baptism for seven-year-olds to discuss the remission of sins. It would emphasize becoming a member of the Christian family. There should be no assumption that the reader is an insider, someone who belongs to a practising

---

Christian family or goes to church. Such comments as 'when you say your prayers...', 'when you were baptized...' should be avoided

4 be capable of being understood by the reader. This means that language levels must be considered, but also that care should be taken not to presume knowledge, e.g. where Jesus was born, who the Romans or Jews were

5 offer an apropriate challenge. All too easily they can simply be story books. The nature of the challenge is to thought and understanding, not to faith, though books should challenge readers to appreciate that Christians take their religion seriously

6 be respectful to different interpretations of Christianity

7 provide awareness of Christian experience. Often the human element of what actions or beliefs mean to Christians is missing

8 be true to Christian experience

9 seek to extend children's understanding

10 deal equitably with race and gender issues (photographs have considerable importance here)

11 avoid narrow nationalism. Christianity is a world wide religion. It should never be presented as only English and white English at that!

12 avoid references to other religions, except where these are necessary. If they cannot be avoided then the full implications should be considered

(e.g. criticisms of Jewish beliefs and practices by Jesus should not ignore the fact that he was a Jew, worshipped in the Temple and synagogues, may have killed his own Passover lamb, and might have been a Pharisee. He was not an outsider hostile to his parent faith)

13 avoid sweeping and simplistic generalizations and stereotypes

14 be attractively produced

15 in short, adopt the same approach to Christianity as one expects to find in books on other religions which are written to help children understand what it means to be, say, a Hindu in terms of world view, belief and practice.

Distancing and luggage

In a nutshell these are the reasons why we find teaching Christianity so difficult:

1 we cannot distance ourselves from the religion. Consequently, our faith or non-faith stance gets in our way, and also in the way of pupils and concerned parents. If we don't want to be accused of 'indoctrination' we do nothing – and so indoctrinate by avoidance. Or we are overwhelmed by the sheer mass of Christianity. Actually, Hinduism may be more varied and equally massive but most of us who teach it are already distanced from it in one way or another

2 the luggage of such things as memories of Bible stories and moral tales intended to make us good, if not give us a faith, for example, are also very much in our minds when we think of how and why to teach Christianity. We must try to leave our luggage behind, as we did when the 'new maths' hit us in the primary classroom or approaches to teaching languages and English changed in the secondary school.

We hope those who can distance themselves and rid themselves of unhelpful luggage will go on to find the rest of the book helpful, but how useful it can be does very much depend upon your attitude. That is why we consider these opening chapters to be important. We end this section with some basic ground rules for teaching about Christianity in maintained schools.

- Teachers should say 'Christians believe...' or 'Christianity teaches...', for example, rather than 'We believe...', or 'When we say our prayers...'.
- In presenting Christianity the teacher should not make disparaging remarks about it.
- Making exaggerated claims for Christianity should be avoided.
- Teachers should avoid imposing their own brand of Christianity, if they have a preference, upon children.
- Teachers should be respectful of pupils' own beliefs and not attempt to undermine them or replace them with their own.
- Comparisons of a value-based nature between one form of Christianity and another, or between Christianity and other religions or non-religious life stances, should be avoided.
- Pupils should clearly understand the reasons which underlie these ground rules and comply with them themselves, so far as is possible, even at Key Stage 1.

PART 2

3 The dimensions of Christianity

In 1968 Professor Ninian Smart published *Secular Education and the Logic of Religion* (Faber), in which he analysed religions in six component parts: ritual, mythological, social, doctrinal, ethical and experiential. These were referred to later in the School's Council Working Paper Number 36. It is entitled *Religious Education in Secondary Schools*, but no one who teaches RE at any stage can ignore it.

The six dimensions of religion have been much discussed. Additions and modifications have been suggested but they have stood the test of time fairly well. We find them of value in organizing our approaches to RE, so we introduce this section on teaching Christianity by outlining them, using Christian examples. (Professor Smart draws on other religions as well.)

We also relate aspects of them to Key Stages 1 and 2. More detail will be provided in later chapters. Before looking at each one, however, we should note that the division is artificial. In most of what we teach all the dimensions will be involved. We will demonstrate this by including baptism as one of the examples throughout.

Ritual

This is a word which can be used to cover any act or practice. Actions vary from closing one's eyes to pray (not a requirement for all Christians) to Sunday worship and lenten fasting. These may seem pointless, formal activities unless they are derived from and related to beliefs. Even at Key Stage 1 teachers should make a link, even if only very simply – for example, by teaching that Christians celebrate Christmas because Jesus is very important and special to them.

The rite of baptism using water derives from the practice of John the Baptist, Jesus, through his disciples (John 4:2), and the early Church (Acts 7:26–40). A visit to a church is an obvious Key Stage 1 way of introducing this dimension, as long as too much is not attempted. It leads to what people do there, when they go and why. These issues lead into the specialness of Sunday and the wish of worshippers to be with God. A simple description of infant baptism could arise naturally from the visit. At Key Stage 2 the ritual actions of worshippers (for example, in the Eucharist or baptism, preparing

Easter foods in some traditions) can be entered into in more detail, and the stories linked with the resurrection on the first day of the week can be read.

Mythological

The much abused word 'myth' simply means the story element in religion. But it reminds believers, and those who study and teach about religions, that the stories have a meaning and that it is their significance that matters. We can argue endlessly about the date when Jesus was born, who the Magi (commonly called the three wise men) were and which star they followed, but the one thing that ultimately matters is what Christianity teaches about Jesus.

Religious stories are ways of conveying beliefs, expressing convictions and challenging or comforting the reader or listener (not always at one and the same time). If we remove these aspects from them, as some attractively produced books for small children do, we emasculate them and reduce them to the level of folk tale or fairy story.

This may mean that some stories should not be used at Key Stage 1 or Key Stage 2. But if we are telling one of the nativity stories, say the visit of the Magi, we should be putting Jesus in the centre of the picture, as all the great artists do, and even using such paintings, perhaps, to demonstrate that Jesus is special for Christians. That is why the Magi came. In what way Jesus is special belongs to Key Stage 2 and Key Stage 3. When visiting a church we can show them the big book which people read, the Bible – the book that focuses upon Jesus.

At Key Stage 1 the baptism story might be no more than telling children that Jesus said that if anyone wanted to join his group of friends they must take a special bath in a river. Some people still do this today, but others simply have water poured over their head in church. (Mention of the sign of the cross is probably Key Stage 2.)

Social

This word is a reminder that religion is not merely a private matter. The Christian is a member of the ecclesia, the community of women and men who, filled by the spirit of God, are called upon to sustain one another and act as yeast and salt (to use analogies made by Jesus) in the life of the world as a whole. Once children have given considerable attention to what it means to belong to a group of friends or be members of a class, a new experience for many of them, they might, at Key Stage 1, be able to explore how Christians help one another and other members of society. Clearly, the ethical and social dimensions are closely related at this stage and would probably be explored together. At Key Stage 2 they might look at biblical and modern local examples of the Church as a community of believers, a family ideally linked by love for Jesus their brother. Baptism is how babies (at Key Stage 1) or believers (Key Stage 2 and beyond) become members of this family; that is why most baptisms take place when the congregation is gathered together on a Sunday.

Doctrinal

These are the teachings of a religion. They range from beliefs about God as creative, loving and forgiving to teachings about eternal life and how individuals can achieve it through faith in Jesus as the divine revelation of God's love.

At Key Stage 1, simple references to believers going to church or praying, because they believe that God loves them and want to be close to him, or the fact that Christians celebrate Jesus' birthday because he is very special to them, may be as far as one can go in laying the foundations for teaching beliefs. At Key Stage 2 those kinds of statements can be amplified with some of the reasons why a relationship with God is considered important by Christians and why Jesus is special. At Key Stage 3 and beyond the doctrinal dimension should be an explicit part of all our teaching, whichever other dimensions are being explored. The challenge to teachers, especially Christians, in looking at doctrines is that of avoiding clichés: 'Jesus saves', 'going to heaven', or even the word 'God', which may actually *mean* nothing. When teachers hear children using them they should not assume that there is no need to unpack them. They should help them explore what the terms mean.

The doctrinal element in baptism at Key Stage 1 may be no more than talking about joining the family of those who think that Jesus is special. The new start might be discussed at Key Stage 2 but the washing away of sins belongs to Key Stage 3 at the earliest.

Ethical

Christianity teaches a code of conduct based on the belief that Christians should follow the commandments and example of Jesus. They should obey the words which he used to sum up the teachings of his Jewish heritage: 'You must love your neighbour as yourself' (Leviticus 19:18). Christians are required to live their lives on this basis. It is difficult enough for those with faith who seek the power of God's love, his grace, to help them. To love one's enemies can seem ridiculous to outsiders who do not share the Christian outlook. The idea of living a new life in which one obeys God is the command placed upon the believer at baptism. It can be discussed at Key Stage 2 in the context of keeping the rules if one joins a club or organization, but it is only at Key Stage 3 that this dimension of baptism can be fully explored explicitly .

At Key Stage 1 we might also be able to invite someone who takes people to Lourdes to visit the school and bring photographs and perhaps even a jumbalance (a specially prepared ambulance for disabled travellers) and talk about their work. Otherwise there may be other local examples which might be used, but personal experience and something tangible are important. The question of motivation – 'why bother?' – could result in the simple statement at this stage: 'because Jesus did it and told his friends that they should follow his example'. At Key Stage 2 some of those exemplary stories which inspire Christians might be told as a follow-up, but note, please, that we did not begin with the story. Actions speak louder than words and it is also good to ring the changes in our approach.

Experiential

This covers two kinds of religious experience. One is that of Jesus in the wilderness or preaching. Something new or original may be said to be involved. The inspiration of biblical writers might be included in this category. The whole life of Jesus, not just his words, adds a distinct dimension to religious experience, Christians would say.

The second is that of St Paul on the Damascus road, or Bernadette at Lourdes, or Martin Luther and John Bunyan, or other Christian believers. Christians in worship and personal prayer share this second kind of experience. They may speak of the presence of the Holy Spirit. This dimension is the essential ingredient of a living faith, both in general terms and particularly. Presumably when this dimension could no longer be found in the religion of ancient Greece, that religion died. Without it worship and personal prayer similarly become lifeless rituals. The experiential element requires religions to be dynamic, possessing power, but for Christians that power is mediated and interpreted through the example of Jesus.

How must it have felt to be invited to become one of Jesus' travelling companions (disciples)? This experience can be explored at Key Stage 1, beginning with the pupils' own experiences of friendship and choosing those they would picnic, play games, camp, go to the zoo with (not always perhaps the same people). The kind of life Jesus was offering his friends might be told to the children. How might they feel if he had asked them to leave home and go with him? At Key Stage 2 we could explore the experiences of Jesus in the wilderness (how should he decide to go about his mission?) or in Gethsemane, or the forgiveness of Peter (John 21), or how Paul felt when Jesus caught up with the hunter of Christians outside Damascus, as well as what Christians derive from praying or going to church. The experiential at Key Stage 1 and Key Stage 2 is very largely going to be related to children's own feelings.

The baptism element may be how parents and family feel at the birth of a new baby, and why they want to take her to be baptized (feelings of wanting to say thank you to God).

It may be seen from this glance at the multidimensional nature of the Christian religion that trying to teach it by concentrating only on one aspect must lead to distortion. Usually this has been done through concentrating only on stories. It can be done, however, by celebrating festivals, especially Christmas, without relating them to doctrine (meaning) or experience (the effect they have on believers), or, in the case of baptism, for example, the things which are actually done (rituals).

In the primary school it is the **ritual** (what Christians do), the **mythological** (the stories they use, often to explain and give basis to the rituals) and the **social** (what belonging to the Christian family means and how it is expressed) dimensions of religion which will form the core of the study of Christianity. In an explicit sense the other areas will be explored later, though they can never be out of the teacher's mind.

Ninian Smart did not specifically mention the overall world view of religions in his dimensions. Perhaps he assumed that the parts put together would make the whole. In our experience this does not happen by accident. Teachers need to understand how members of religions make sense of the world. Otherwise their beliefs, values and above all their practices make little sense at all. We must now, therefore, outline the Christian world view.

4 How Christians view the world

Introduction

One of the most important ways in which we can ensure that the study of a religion is a legitimate, educational exercise is to make a genuine attempt to understand each religion in its own terms. Every religion offers a very distinctive way of making sense of the world – what might be called its 'world view'. The value and excitement of Religious Education lies in its ability to introduce children to the fact that human beings understand the world in different ways and that the best chance we have of understanding our fellow human beings is to understand their world view. It is therefore vital that, for instance, we approach Islam from a Muslim point of view, not a Christian one. It is equally vital that we try to understand Christianity by discovering its distinctive world view. The history of the teaching of Christianity in our schools, as discussed in the previous chapter, makes this very difficult. In many ways, it is easier even for the non-specialist to distinguish the *distinctive* practices and beliefs of Islam than it is to do the same for Christianity. Because of our cultural and educational background, nearly all of us are too 'close' to Christianity to see it. As we saw in Chapter 3, we have to make the mental effort to distance ourselves from Christianity in order to see it as a world religion with a very distinctive way of making sense of the world. In the same way, we have to remind ourselves that the pupils we teach cannot understand Christianity as a distinctive religious tradition unless they are taught about it. We cannot assume a knowledge of Christianity in them any more than in ourselves.

In this chapter, therefore, we are going to try and explore what could be meant by a Christian world view and how an understanding of it could be applied to the classroom.

Developing an understanding

Religious belief is a very complex subject and we are not suggesting that children should be taught Christian doctrine as such until at least Key Stage 4. We would argue, however, that, just like any other area of the curriculum – Science, English etc. – the teacher needs to understand the concepts involved and then present children with approaches and activities which lay the foundations for an understanding of these complex issues and concepts when they reach a later stage in their education.

We will therefore isolate the central aspects of a distinctively Christian world view and then consider how this could permeate the way in which we, as teachers, present the beliefs and practices of Christianity to pupils. The most basic idea that we need to get across is that rituals like the Eucharist and stories like the Christmas and Easter stories can only be properly *understood* – regardless of whether we *believe* them or not – if they are seen in their context of a Christian world view.

A simple golden rule to follow, therefore, is, whenever dealing with Christian beliefs and practices, always to present them as 'Christians believe...Christians say that...' rather than 'we do...we say...' etc. Just to get into the habit of thinking in this way makes a fair and educational approach to the teaching of Christianity as a world religion more possible. (With Key Stage 1 children, it may not be appropriate to use the actual term 'Christian' – instead you might need to say something like: 'The people who go to that church...' – just try to avoid the word 'we'.)

Central aspects of the Christian world view

1 The centrality of Jesus

Christianity is about Jesus. The figure of Jesus has become a very familiar one to all those who live in a culture based on Christianity. Furthermore, Jesus is respected as a great teacher or prophet in many traditions other than Christianity. Muslims respect Jesus as a great prophet; many Hindus regard him as a great teacher; many Humanists or those who are simply unwilling to accept the religious Christian position regard Jesus as a very good person who is worthy of imitation.

In view of this it is often difficult – but educationally very important – to distinguish distinctively Christian beliefs about Jesus. To Christians, Jesus is not just a great teacher, prophet and example; he is the revelation of God in a unique way. As well as having lived as a person 2,000 years ago, he is also the second person of the Trinity and is present in the lives of believers of the Risen Lord. Christians believe that they can know God through a very personal relationship with Jesus. This is at the very heart of Christianity and explains many of its distinctive features. This belief is linked with the other three aspects of a Christian world view.

2 The Incarnation

Central to Christianity is the belief that God became 'incarnate' or 'in the flesh' through the life of Jesus. This leads to the Christian belief that Jesus is both fully human and fully divine – a belief unique to Christianity. The fact that Christianity claims that God has been revealed through a person, rather than a book or a covenant, explains some of the very personal imagery used by Christians to describe God.

3 The Trinity

The belief that Jesus is the Incarnation is linked with the Christian belief in the Trinity. Christianity is a monotheistic religion – i.e. it believes in one God – but it claims that the one God is known in three 'persons': Father, Son and Holy Spirit. This phrase indicates the many ways in which God is to be understood, and reflects beliefs that God is both transcendent and immanent; that is, that God is both 'out there' and present in the immediate experience of the believer.

The 'Father' aspect of God relates to God as Creator and Judge of all humanity. The concept of the world as God's creation is central to Christianity. The 'Son' aspect is known through the life, death and resurrection of Jesus Christ. The term Holy Spirit reminds Christians that God is active in the work and worship of the Church and in the life of individuals. Many Christians also believe that through the Holy Spirit God is present throughout the world.

4 The resurrection

Another central belief unique to Christianity is belief in the resurrection of Jesus. This is the claim that Jesus triumphed over death by being raised three days after his crucifixion. The Christian belief in resurrection is not the same as saying that Jesus was 'brought back to life' in the way that Jairus' daughter (Mark 5:35–43) or Lazarus (John 11:1–44) was. These would eventually have to die some time in the future. Christians believe that Jesus truly died and then rose into eternal life. The Gospels give accounts of Jesus being revealed to his disciples in his risen body which was 'real' (e.g. Luke 24: 36–43 and John 20:19–29) but not bound by the limits of a physical body (e.g. Luke 24:13–31 and John 20:26). Christians believe that Jesus' bodily presence then 'ascended' into Heaven. The significance of these beliefs for Christians today is that they therefore claim that Jesus is as alive today as he was 2,000 years ago, and can be known to believers as 'the Risen Lord'.

5 The concept of sin and forgiveness

All religions can be seen as attempts to make sense of the human condition, as responses to the human experience that we are not as we 'ought' to be. Christians explain the experience of human dissatisfaction and failure to live as they feel they should in terms of 'sin' and 'fallen' humanity. Christians believe that because of their pride and disobedience, humans have separated themselves from God. They refer to this as the Fall. The story of the Fall is given in Genesis chapter 3. Some Christians understand this as an historical event, others as a story which expresses the truth of the human condition in its fallen state. As a result of the Fall, Christians believe, humans are in a state of sin. Sin can best be understood as alienation from God. The Greek word used in the Bible means 'missing the mark'. Because humans are created by God, they can find true peace and fulfilment only in relationship with God, yet their own sin makes this impossible. This, according to Christianity, is the terrible predicament of humankind, which it is powerless to correct. Only God can restore the relationship and remove sin. This possibility of renewed relationship has, Christians believe, taken place through the life, death and resurrection of Jesus. Jesus, as fully human and fully divine, bridged the gap caused by human sin to make possible a full relationship with God. Jesus took on the sin of humanity and paid its price through his suffering and death, on behalf of all humanity. As a result, humans need to accept that Jesus died for their sin and experience their sense of dependency in God and they will be forgiven and saved or redeemed in order to participate in a full relationship with God. The concept of forgiveness is therefore very important in Christian belief, and this understanding of the human condition is central to a distinctively Christian world view. The importance of Jesus' death as the means of atonement for sin and of the possibility of forgiveness is reflected in the central symbol of the Christian tradition – the cross, because Jesus died on a cross.

Teaching suggestions

Key Stage 1

It would be inappropriate to attempt to discuss these complex doctrines with young children – but it is very appropriate to lay the foundations of an understanding of these beliefs for later years. This can be done by presenting the scripture and practices of Christianity as special to a particular group of believers, and by showing that they are used by those believers to express what they find to be true. Children can be introduced to the idea that Christians believe that God created the world and that people can only be truly happy when close to God. It is important, however, that these beliefs are presented as a particular view of the world, and not as an assumption which children are required to share.

Key Stage 2

By this stage, pupils can be introduced to more specific beliefs through an exploration of the practices of the Christian community. Children can begin to understand what Christians believe by learning about what they 'do' – e.g. celebrate Easter and Christmas, go to church, read the Bible, become baptized etc. – and appreciating the importance of these practices for their adherents.

Key Stage 3

By the end of Key Stage 3, pupils should be aware of the distinctively Christian beliefs about God and Jesus – i.e. the concepts of the Trinity and the belief that Jesus is both fully human and fully divine. These beliefs can be presented through a deeper understanding of Christian festivals, practices and worship.

Key Stage 4

By the end of Key Stage 4, pupils should be aware of the beliefs expressed in the major Christian creeds. They should also be able to show how these beliefs affect Christians' understanding of the world and humanity.

Issues

When we attempt to isolate the distinctive beliefs of Christianity, we appreciate just how complex they are. Because most of us are so 'close' to Christianity, if only because of our cultural and educational background, we often do not 'see' what the central and distinctive doctrines of Christianity are. Only then do we realize that they involve so many paradoxes and difficult concepts.

It has been argued that Buddhism, for instance, should not be presented to pupils until the sixth form because its philosophy is too difficult. By that argument, neither should Christianity. We would argue that the Christian world view can be taught from Key Stage 1 in the developmental way we have tried to present in this chapter. (Incidentally, we would argue the same for Buddhism.)

Further reading

The Christians, P McKenzie, SPCK, 1988. Relates the diversity of practices and belief to phenomena and concepts.

5 Story

Introduction

'Is it true or is it just a story?'

This comment, likely to be heard from pupils in the reception class right through to the sixth form, reflects the way in which our modern western society devalues the role of story in making sense of the world. In a religious world view, however, story is a powerful and meaningful way of expressing truth. In order to help children understand this, we have consciously to counter the dominant message which they receive. They live in a culture which teaches, directly or indirectly, that the only truth is that which can be proved empirically. A story is only 'true', therefore, if it gives an accurate account of historical events as they happened. This is a very limited understanding of what the 'truth' might be.

When Professor Ninian Smart pioneered the 'Religious Studies' approach to understanding religion, he argued that the student should be aware of the many dimensions of a religious tradition (see Chapter 3). One such dimension is, he said, the mythical. By this he meant that all religions tell stories or provide narratives to explain the truth as they see it. The fact that the term 'myth' has a very different meaning in everyday language again reflects the derogatory way in which our society regards story. To the person in the street a myth means an untruth – even a deliberate lie put forward to deceive others. We believe that unless children are helped to see beyond such a limited understanding of myth and story they are unlikely to be able to understand the importance of the Bible to Christianity or, indeed, to understand Christianity at all. We would go further and say that it is an important part of a child's aesthetic and spiritual education as a whole to appreciate that, in most cultures other than our own, the terms 'truth' and 'story' are not mutually exclusive. Religious Education offers a marvellous opportunity to help children 're-learn' the power and importance of story in the human experience.

Stories in the classroom

We are arguing, therefore, that pupils need to explain the concept of story as a foundation for understanding the Bible and other religious stories in

Christianity. Such an exploration should lead children to realize that the appropriate question to ask about a religious story is not 'did it happen?' but 'what does it mean?'

All this is not to say that the children must accept the meaning of the story as true for them – that is entirely their own personal decision. What we do hope, however, is that they attempt to understand what the story means to the believers who cherish it and therefore what 'truth' means to them.

To support this view, we quote from a Christian biblical scholar:

'There is a serious effort in much recent biblical scholarship to come to grips with the biblical narrative as a story – which means listening to what it says about God and ourselves, apart from questions of how accurately the narrative reflects the actual events of the past... The figure of Ruth moves us whether the figure in the story is based on an actual person or not. The character of the forgiving father in the story of "the prodigal son" is powerful and effective as an image of God even if he is not patterned after an actual historical father...

The Jewish and Christian communities of faith through the centuries have lived off these stories and in the light of these stories, and it is within one or another of these communities of faith that these stories have exercised their claims on each of us believers. We have no immediate access to the circumstances which gave birth to the biblical stories. It is not the inaugural events which claim and sustain us, but the *stories*. If historical research demonstrates them to be historically inaccurate, it nevertheless remains true that successive communities of believing peoples have accepted them. Generations have found in these stories (as they are, and not in some critically reconstructed history "behind" them) affirmations that shaped their understanding of what it meant to live in 900BCE or 500BCE or 1600CE in the presence of the Lord God. For believers living at various points in history, the tradition "rang true".

The tradition "rang true" in their own experience and enabled them to develop a self-understanding and a lifestyle. It was the tradition as received which accomplished this, not the past-as-it-actually-was.'
(From *The Quest for the Historical Israel*, George W Ramsey, SCM Press, 1981)

Having said this, we must acknowledge that many Christians do believe that the authority of biblical stories lies in their historical accuracy. Children need to be aware of this – but this does not detract from what has gone before. Nearly all Christians accept the stories as 'true' or meaningful, whether or not they understand them as historically accurate – and this is what pupils need to appreciate.

Finally, we will need to consider the use of a particular type of Christian story: the parable. We would argue that the parables which Jesus told are marvellous examples of the power of story – and yet, unfortunately, the way in which they are presented in the classroom does not always reflect this. The results of biblical scholarship which explores the nature and function of the parables may help to rectify this situation. Scholars argue that the parables as Jesus originally told them were not the 'moral tales' they are usually presented as today. They further argue that they were not told as allegories – that is, stories in which each element represents something – and did not need to be 'interpreted'. Instead, they claim, the parables were stories which presented the hearers with a familiar situation with which they could identify. Because of this identification the hearers were then led by the story to face a challenge and make a response. The parable, therefore, raised questions for the hearers rather than giving them answers. Because Jesus' parables were so powerful and immediate, they related very closely to the everyday lives of the 1st century Israeli peasants to whom they were addressed. Inevitably, therefore, when the stories are removed from their original contexts, they need some interpretation for a new audience. The process of doing this, however, is rather like trying to explain a joke – their original impact is automatically lost. The scholars argue that by recreating the original settings of the parables, it is possible to appreciate the sort of challenges and questions Jesus presented to his audiences. Christians who follow this process believe that the challenges presented by the earthly Jesus then are the same as those posed by the Risen Lord today.

If we look at some examples of this approach to the parables, we might better understand what the scholars mean.

One interesting example is the story usually known as the Dishonest Steward in Luke 16:1–13. This is not a very well known story because it does not lend itself to the traditional interpretations. The story itself tells of a rascal who has been working as a steward – a sort of 'farm manager' for a rich boss. The boss has realized that this steward is not doing his job properly, so asks to see the books because he is going to give the steward the sack. The steward is panic-stricken – with no unemployment benefit his only option seems to be hard manual labour or begging. He then makes a plan to help his situation and instantly puts it into action in the brief time he has before presenting the books to his boss. He quickly summons the people who owe his boss and alters the bills, so that it looks as if they owe much less than they really do. In this way, the steward has made some friends who will be prepared to look after him when he loses his job.

The story itself ends at verse 7. The next six verses are unsuccessful attempts to interpret this story in order to provide a moral or doctrinal message!

Scholars argue that the original story offers an analogy to the hearer, even though it has as its 'hero' a rather immoral rascal. They suggest that this story about the cheeky exploits of the steward might have been the local gossip at the time. The context of the story reflects completely the agricultural life of the original hearers. The scholars say that the situation faced by the steward – the need to make an urgent decision immediately, on which all may depend – is one which is presented by many of Jesus' parables: for instance, the parable of the Hidden Treasure and Pearl of Great Price (Matthew 13:45–6). Jesus is challenging his hearers to identify with this situation.

Another example of this kind of challenge is presented in the story of the Great Supper (Matthew 22:1–14, Luke 14:14–24). In this story the hearers would recognize the familiar situation in which a wedding feast was being prepared and the guests were informed that they should be ready to come when all was complete. In this case, however, the guests are not ready – so the holder of the feast brings in people off the street. This clever twist in the story reflects the fact that many of Jesus' fellow Jews were complaining about his teaching (and example) that even the worst sinners were being offered forgiveness and entry into the Kingdom of God. The challenge of the story is that people who had an invitation turned it down, and now people who did not know that they were invited are coming in. The account of this parable in Matthew and Luke is particularly interesting because it highlights the very different ways in which the two Gospels interpret the same story. The writer of Matthew's Gospel was concerned to convince the Jewish community that Christians were the true Israel. He emphasized the idea that those who believed themselves to be invited would not be included. He therefore inserted two stories into the original parable. The first (verses 5 to 7) provides an allegory which states that the destruction of Jerusalem was a punishment for the rejection of Jesus. The second (verses 11 to 13) describes the punishment of someone who turns up without a wedding garment – an obvious addition, in view of the fact that the original story tells us the guests were brought in from the street! There is some debate about what this means; most scholars believe it refers to the garment provided by baptism.

The writer of Luke was concerned to introduce Christianity to the Gentile world. He therefore emphasizes the offer of an invitation to outsiders. In his version, the servants go out twice – first to the outcastes within the city, and then to those outside who represent the Gentiles.

We will now consider how the concept of 'story' can be developed throughout a pupil's school life and how this would relate to the understanding of Christian stories.

A list of Synoptic Parables

Matthew only

Tares and wheat 13:24
Hidden treasure 13:44
Pearl 13:45+
Drag net 13:47
Unmerciful servant 18:23+
Labourers in vineyard 20:1+
Two sons 21:28+
Wise and foolish maidens 25:1+
Sheep and goats 25:31+

Mark only

Seed growing secretly 4:26+

Matthew and Luke

The leaven (Matthew 13:33,
  Luke 13:20)
The lost sheep (Matthew 18:12,
  Luke 1)
{ Great supper (Luke 14:16+)
  Marriage of king's son
    (Matthew 22:1+)
{ Pounds (Luke 19:13+)
  Talents (Matthew 25:14+)

Luke only

Two debtors 7:41+
Good Samaritan 10:30+
Importunate friend 11:5+
Rich fool 12:16+
Barren fig-tree 13:6+
Tower builder 14:28+
Rash king 14:31+
Lost coin 15:8+
Lost son 15:11+
Dishonest steward 16:1+
Rich man and Lazarus 16:19+
The farmer and his man or
  unprofitable servants 17:7+
Unjust judge 18:1+
Pharisee and tax collector 18:9+

Matthew, Mark and Luke

Sower (Matthew 13:1, Mark 4:2+,
  Luke 8:4+)
Mustard seed (Matthew 13:31+,
  Mark 4:30+, Luke 13:18+)
Wicked tenants (Matthew 21:33,
  Mark 12, Luke 20:9+)

Teaching suggestions

Key Stage 1

Very young children seem to have an innate appreciation of the power of story, but this is 'educated' out of them, often even before they reach reception class. Children do have to learn the difference between 'fact' and 'fiction' – but this should not automatically be equated with the difference between 'truth' and 'falsehood'. Story-telling and story-making is an essential part of good primary school education, but we would argue that children should realize from the start that there are different types of story. If children are presented with fairy-stories, Roald Dahl stories and Bible stories alongside one another with no comment and explanation, it is perhaps not surprising that they do not appreciate the different functions of story. We would argue, first of all, that religious stories should always be told in context, even if this only means that they are introduced by a phrase such as: 'Here is a story told by some people because it is very important to them...'. The children should not be made to feel that it must be important to *them*, but that they should respect it because of its importance to others.

To achieve this, however, we would argue that at this stage there should be more emphasis on presenting non-Biblical stories which help children see that stories can have an important meaning – regardless of whether they reflect historical fact.

In order to convey the role of 'stories with meaning' the teacher could borrow an idea from Steiner education and light a candle to burn during the telling of the story. While the candle burns, no one else should speak but the story-teller. When the candle goes out, the audience can discuss the story. The teacher should not direct this discussion with 'factual' questions, but allow the children to say what they liked or did not like about the story, and thereby move into what they thought the story *meant*. If young children are allowed to respond to stories in this way, the result can be some remarkable comments and insights.

This process should also help children realize that some stories – valuable though they are – are not 'candle' stories. Teachers can use any story which they personally find worthwhile, but we recommend at the end of the chapter some of the stories that we enjoy using. Please note that 'candle stories' can also be very entertaining and humourous – for instance, the stories of David McKee and Michael Foreman.

Key Stage 2

The practice of telling stories with meaning or 'candle stories' can continue into this stage, but in addition, the teacher can introduce more stories from the Bible. So, for example, children can hear some favourite Christian stories about Jesus and be encouraged to ask questions like: 'What does this story tell us about Jesus? Why do Christians tell this story?' When they hear the wonderful stories about Moses, Abraham, Joseph, etc. they can ask: 'What does this story tell us about the way in which God acts to affect people's lives?' Instead of the common practice of telling a Bible story and then doing nothing – or at best drawing a picture – children should begin to explore the reasons why the story was told and remembered and why it is so important to those who cherish it.

Key Stage 3

By this stage, pupils should be able to build on the foundations laid earlier and begin to appreciate the difficult concept that different people tell different stories in order to say what they think is 'true'. One exciting way of exploring this is to consider a variety of creation stories (see the recommended material at the end of this book). The pupils will almost certainly have met the Genesis stories at Key Stage 2, but now they could explore the meaning of these stories in more depth (see pages 60–4).

Another way in which to deepen an understanding of biblical stories is to examine the stories that Jesus told as parables. We discussed the understanding of these stories in some detail in the introduction to this chapter. Unfortunately, the power and vibrancy of these stories are too often lost in their dry repetition as 'moral tales'. One way to recapture their original excitement is to involve the pupils in role play. We would argue that this approach is particularly relevant to an understanding of the parables, because it is in keeping with the function of the parable itself: that is, to draw the hearer in to identify with the situation portrayed in the story. By identifying with the father, older son or younger son in the story of the Lost Son (Luke 15:11–32), children can better appreciate the challenge that Jesus was offering to the hearers of his day.

The work of biblical scholars suggests that Jesus was offering a challenge to his fellow Jews, who could not accept his teaching that God was offering forgiveness and entry into his kingdom to *all* who would accept, even those who had previously been sinners. The story of the lost son provides a powerful analogy to this situation, when the older son's angry reaction to his younger brother's welcome and acceptance by a forgiving father is easy to understand and even be sympathetic with. By acting out this story with children and asking them how they feel in the role they are playing, these peaceful, theological issues are being explored and the original challenge of the parable is being brought home.

The use of drama and exercises such as 'imagine you are writing a newspaper report' are ways of bringing Bible stories alive for pupils. We would, however, offer a word of caution against using these approaches with biblical narratives, because they can convey the message that the 'value' of the story lay in historical events rather than in the 'meaning' of the story – as Ramsey writes above. This need not preclude their use completely, however. If, for instance, the story of Jesus and Zacchaeus (Luke 19:1–10) is presented as a story which Christians remembered because it taught them what Jesus was like – then drama can be used to bring out the meaning of that story. For example, pupils can consider what the response of the crowd would be: what would they say? How would Zacchaeus react – what would he be thinking?

In order to help children understand this story they really need to be informed about the relevant background. Once they appreciate how much tax collectors were hated by their fellow Jews because they worked for the enemy – the Roman occupiers – the significance of Jesus' acceptance of such a person makes more sense. Likewise, if they realize that the tax collectors could claim as much commission as they liked for themselves, and could therefore become very rich, Zacchaeus' decision to give this all up would have more impact.

Key Stage 4

If pupils are properly prepared, then by Key Stage 4 they should be in a position to tackle some of the more challenging aspects of the Christian story. For example, they could consider the meaning of the resurrection stories. Norman Perrin, a Christian scholar, described these stories as 'literary expressions of what it means to say that "Jesus is risen"'. The theological meaning behind the birth narratives and the ascension story can also be considered. The theology involved here – the belief in Jesus as the Risen Lord, the Incarnation and the second person of the Trinity – are central to any possible understanding of the Christian world view. We would argue that it is only through a proper appreciation of the way in which Christian stories convey these beliefs that any such understanding is possible.

Further reading

For the teacher

Tell me a story: story and RE, Maurice Lynch, West London RE Centre, (the address is given in Appendix 2).
The Quest for the Historical Israel, George W Ramsey, SCM Press, 1981.

For the classroom

Key Stage 1
These books are not explicitly religious but raise many of the issues to which religions provide answers.

Amazing Grace, Mary Hoffman, Frances Lincoln, 1991. The self-image of an Afro-Caribbean girl who wants to play Peter Pan. The support she receives and the obstacles she overcomes.
Dinosaurs and all that Rubbish, M Foreman, Hamish Hamilton, 1972. The dinosaurs return to clear up the mess made by humans. Ecology and creation related.
Frederick, Leo Lionni, Abelard. Frederick the mouse spends his time musing on the wonders of the world and neglects to stock his larder against the arrival of winter.

Frederick's Tales, Leo Lionni, Anderson Press, 1986. Addresses many areas of human relationships.

Fish is Fish, Leo Lionni, Abelard-Schuman, 1972. A fish discovers the world beyond his pond from stories told by his friend the frog. An introduction to the difficult concept of different ways of looking at the world.

John Brown, Rose and the Midnight Cat, Jenny Wagner, Kestrel, 1977. The effect which a stray cat has on a close friendship.

Mama, do you love me?, Barbara Joose, Little, Brown and Company, 1992. A child tests his mother's love and discovers that she would love him however dreadful he became, even a monster who frightened her. Comes as close as anything to the Christian concept of God's forgiving love.

Nicholas, where have you been?, Leo Lionni, Anderson Press, 1987. A conflict and hatred story and the solution. Could be frightening.

One World, M Foreman, Anderson Press, 1990. Children make their mini-world and think about responsibility to the larger world they inhabit.

Tusk Tusk, David McKee, Anderson Press, 1978. A story of hatred between black and white elephants. Amusing but clear treatment of issues of prejudice and intolerance.

Key Stage 2

Brother Eagle, Sister Sky, Susan Jeffers, Puffin, 1993. Chief Seattle's view of the world is implicitly contrasted with the typical view of westerners.

Leila, Sue Alexander, Hamish Hamilton, 1988. A Muslim girl helps her father cope with the loss of her brother (also Key Stage 3).

Panda's Puzzle and his Voyage of Discovery, M Foreman, Hamish Hamilton, 1977. Is he a black bear with white bits or a white bear with black bits? Eventually he discovers that he is himself!

Speaking of God, Trevor Dennis, Triangle, 1992. A thought-provoking telling of biblical stories. Plenty to discuss (also Key Stage 3 and upwards).

Tales of the Early World, Ted Hughes, Faber, 1990. Witty accounts of how the world might have come to be.

The Sea People, Jorg Muller and Jorg Steiner, Gollancz, 1982. The story of the contrasting lifestyles and outlooks of the inhabitants of two islands.

The Selfish Giant, Oscar Wilde, Puffin, 1982. An illustrated version of the story about the power of love.

The Whales' Song, Dyan Sheldon and Gary Blythe, Hutchinson, 1988. Grandma and Uncle Frederick tell very different stories about whales. Lily goes down to the jetty to find out for herself.

6 Active learning and the use of artefacts

I hear and I forget, I read and I remember, I do and I understand

A teacher took a case containing a broad-brimmed hat and light dress, sunglasses, a rosary, a picture of the Pope and a guide book to Rome written in Italian and English into school. She asked her 9-year-olds to open it and try to decide where she had been. The hat, dress and shades enabled them to work out that the place must have been hot. The guide book said 'Rome' and they were able to find it in an atlas with a bit of help. No one recognized the Pope or a rosary; that is where the teacher had to take over, but the children were now interested enough to want to know more. The teacher helped them find out about the Pope and about St Peter and the catacombs and other stories about early Christians in Rome. A visit by a nun provided an expert explanation of the rosary, its use and its story.

This hands-on approach can be taken to RE at any age level, in fact we often give students an artefact when they arrive in college and ask them to discover what it is and how it is used so that they can explain it to their peers the following week.

Story-telling and writing have always been the stock in trade of real education and especially of RE and History. Those of us who are teachers probably enjoyed it, and it worked successfully, as did writing essays as the one follow-up exercise. But what of our former classmates, who didn't benefit from the approach? The best some of them could be offered was often the opportunity to draw a picture. They are better examples than we are, and far more numerous! Story-telling also gives a feeling of safety. Tell a story from the Bible and you can say that you have fulfilled your obligation to teach RE, just as teaching tables satisfied the angst of some Maths teachers. This may please the few but often vocal parents who ask their children what they did in RE today, but just as rote learning failed most children when it came to thinking mathematically, so story-telling has limited success in helping children to understand religion. We consider that the use of story in RE is still important, to the extent that we have given it a chapter of its own. We argue, however, that story exploration will be only one of many approaches which we use in studying religion. We hope that they will be used in conjunction with other suggestions made in this section whenever possible, not apart from skills, attitudes and concepts and with artefacts also being used to explore their meaning.

Artefacts

Many of the suggestions in this book will involve the use of artefacts.

In a Year 2 or even Year 1 classroom you might notice, during a visit, some children who seem to be bathing a baby doll. One of them is wearing the kind of clothes a minister puts on when taking a service. In fact, it's a baptism. In this example the children are using artefacts: vestments, doll and portable font. There is nothing particularly new in that.

What is new about the use of artefacts is that they are becoming respectable teaching aids and are seen to have a worth of their own. The doll was to be put away as soon as possible. It was one of those childish things which children had to be weaned from, for the real educational diet was book learning. Museums were, more often than not, cases of objects to be seen but never touched. Artefacts were used as points of reference in the story. Artefacts may have been used to help settle the pupils down, but after five minutes they would be back into the same old groove.

The discovery of artefacts by RE teachers is related to a broadening of the syllabus and changes in approaches to teaching. Until very recently the only artefact needed was the Bible, but that was not regarded as an artefact. The object had no worth; it was the Word which it contained that was important, and that was no artefact, something made by human hands – it was divine revelation. Besides pandering to childish immaturity an artefact would deflect attention from what really mattered.

Now, although the Bible has a proper and very important place in the teaching of Christianity, we teach more than biblical knowledge and theology. We teach the context in which the Bible has meaning: Christian worship. That requires a visit to that largest local religious artefact of all, a church, to find out what it looks like, why it is there, what happens in it and who goes to it. In that church pupils will see a Bible placed in a position of prominence. It may be very large and heavy – a sure sign of importance for younger children.

One of the biggest changes in primary scool teaching is active learning. Instead of being the passive child we were expected to be, listening to stories in History, Geography, RE or Science, or watching the teacher illustrate the story in Arithmetic, by writing on the blackboard, nowadays children move about, explore, find out, handle things and are encouraged to ask questions. It is believed, quite correctly, that children learn by doing. Artefacts fit best into an active learning and discovery context. It can be an abuse simply to take an artefact into the classroom to awaken interest and then to put it away in a drawer or the pocket. It is also a waste to use something which is stimulating in itself only to gain control and create curiosity. The interest aroused should be permitted to develop momentum.

One example might be provided to illustrate this. In the rear window of the car in front you may see this symbol.

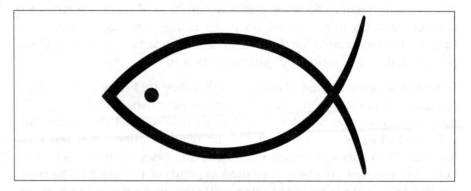

You may carry one yourself, in the lapel of a jacket or on your own car. It represents a fish. What can it say to the person who sees it?

- Its owner is a Christian.
- The fish is an older symbol than the cross. It is found, together with loaves of bread, painted on walls in the catacombs of Rome and on a mosaic. There may be a link with Jesus as the 'bread of life', (John 6:35) and with the Lord's Supper.
- The fish was used by early Christians, perhaps as a secret sign, marked on the ground in response to a stranger who asked them: 'Can you tell me the Way?' If they were merely looking for directions the mark would go unnoticed. If the questioner was a person of the Way, as Christianity was called (Jesus said: 'I am the way' – John 14:6), they would see it and be enabled to make contact with the Christian community.
- The fish meant Jesus. The Greek word for fish is ιχθυς (the Greek initials standing for Jesus Christ God's Son Saviour).
- The fish is important at several places in the Gospels. Jesus called his fisherman disciples to be 'fishers of men' (Mark 1:17). The five thousand were fed on loaves and fishes (Mark 8:38). One of the resurrection narratives describes Jesus cooking fish (John 21:13). The fear of the disciples who thought they were seeing a ghost when the risen Jesus appeared to them was dispelled when, at his request, they gave him some fish to eat (Luke 24:42). Fish and bread were, of course, the staple diet of Jews, especially in the Galilee region of Palestine, but for the members of

the developing Church its symbolic and reassuring meaning was what mattered.

So much significance in one small artefact! Can we somehow communicate it by letting children handle the car sticker or the lapel pin?

At Key Stage 1 the fish can be introduced as a reminder of Jesus who, they already know, is a special person important to Christians. It can be used to demonstrate the function of a secret sign. (The metaphor of 'fishers of men' will probably be lost on children at this stage.)

If the feeding of the five thousand is used, it should stress the idea of Jesus as provider. It is he, not the boy, who is central to the story, and there is no evidence of other people in the crowd being shamed into sharing what they had brought but hidden under their cloaks.

If children are told some of the resurrection stories at this stage, they could include those which the followers of Jesus might remember whenever they saw the sign of the fish.

At Key Stage 2 secret signs and hiding in the catacombs should stimulate the imagination. Nero's persecution and Christians being thrown to wild beasts explain why secrecy was important. Feelings of being a Christian in this kind of world could be examined, especially through role-play. The need for faith and real commitment could be included with older pupils. Key Stage 2 is a long developmental stage.

The community stories mentioned at Key Stage 1 should now certainly be examined in the context of giving anxious Christians reassurance.

Key Stage 3 is the stage at which the the word ιχθυς and its meaning for Christians can be learned. The link with the Lord's Supper should be made. A study of Christian symbols – light, the cross, the dove – should be undertaken if it has not been done already.

At Key Stage 4 the pupil should be in a position to say what might come into the mind of a Christian who sees the sign of the fish on the rear window of the car in front.

We see from this example that the artefact does not replace the story but can anchor it in the imagination.

Artefacts tend to have two meanings. The first is immediate, the second distant. Take a crucifix, for example. First, there is what we see: a man hanging limp and dead from a cross-shaped piece of wood to which he is held by nails through his hands and feet. There is a story connected with it. That story can be told. The crucifix, however, points to something else; it has a more profound meaning. It is not just a dreadful reminder of what people are capable of doing to other people and did 2,000 years ago to Jesus. It speaks of the nature of God, as Christians understand it. It poses two questions for the teacher. First: when do we use it? At what stage of development can children cope with the immediate aspects? Secondly: do we actually proceed to the more distant and deeper significance? The same teacher isn't going to be the person to answer both questions, because a number of years lies between exploring the immediate and examining the distant, but artefacts are not being used properly if both are not dealt with eventually. What applies to the crucifix is also true of the baby doll used in the simulated baptism. There is the joyful welcoming of the baby into the home and a feeling of thankfulness to God which some people have and wish to express. This is the immediate meaning of the baby. More distantly, baptism says something about the nature of humanity and the nature of God, the whole issue of forgiveness and the possibility of a fresh start. That is something that the children simulating a baptism couldn't possibly understand. The teacher should decide when to use a particular artefact and how far to go with the class, but should also be aware of what more there is to explore.

Artefacts need to be anchored to the child's experience and the religion's world view – otherwise they are merely quaint, perhaps interesting irrelevances. Most Christian artefacts can be touched and examined, unlike some of those belonging to other religions, but we would ask that children do so with respect.

Artefact and story often enhance one another, as we saw in the fish emblem example. The communion table or altar and the vessels used in celebrating the sacrament go hand in hand with the narrative of the Last Supper (not all of it, but the parts children can understand from their own experience of friendship expressed through a shared meal). We shouldn't be eager to be didactic; rather, we should encourage children to be deductive and provide them with potentially 'penny-dropping' situations. So we begin with a table and a meal at home and experiences of special family occasions, such as parties; perhaps a rarely used table cloth, the best china and cutlery. (As a child we may have known that there was someone 'important' coming because the table was laid in the dining room.) Next we ask why we have special family occasions with a meal as the focus. Then we can move into the special meal which Christians share. A visit to a church to see the table/altar and vessels could follow and then the story of Jesus' last meal with his friends. Its importance in sustaining the fearful Christians in Rome could be dealt with and, at Key Stage 3 or Key Stage 4, why Roman Catholic priests risked their lives in Elizabethan England to ensure that believers could receive the sacrament.

Teaching Christianity is about what Christians believe and do and not our personal reactions and beliefs. The majority of Christians make considerable use of artefacts.

Finally, there is a need to use the correct names; this is a way of showing respect. To refer to the rosary used by Roman Catholics as 'worry beads' is disrespectful. Chidren are often much more ready than we are to learn new words, including the names of artefacts or people, and are certainly capable of doing so.

Obtaining artefacts used to be a great problem; it is now made easier through such companies as Articles of Faith. The address is given in Appendix 2. The purpose of particular artefacts and how they are used may be discovered from reading some of the books listed in the bibliography, but if in doubt there is always the possibility of inviting a member of the faith to come and explain them and their value to the believer.

Active learning

It is difficult to distinguish between active learning and activities – many of the suggestions include both. Activities can often be a form of stimulus and an opportunity for thought and reflection.

Important examples are:

Visits

All children should make several educational visits to churches during their school lives. If one of them can be when worship is taking place so much the better, but we realize that this may not be possible. However, eucharists, baptism and other services do sometimes take place during the week and it may be possible to sit in on them as observers. For this to be possible it is necessary first of all to educate the children, perhaps their parents, the worshippers and the worship-leader. Children and parents (who should be informed by letter) need to know that they are observers. Sometimes parents who are not church-goers become anxious that the visit is intended to indoctrinate, or make them feel guilty that they do not go to church. With skill it might be possible to invite one or two such parents to be helpers. If the visit goes well they will be reassured and could become your greatest supporters - and all RE teachers need friends! It may also be useful in giving children confidence. For many of them a church is a strange and possibly threatening place.

Observation skills have to be taught and developed, probably through watching TV programmes (not necessarily in RE) and on other school journeys. Even in higher education we often expect students to be able to observe an activity and analyze it, only to discover that they don't know what to look for or how to observe. This is particularly true of analyzing or reflecting upon photographs or videos.

If you are attending an act of worship of any kind the minister should be seen and helped to understand your educational purpose. The minister can then prepare the congregation or the family, if it is a baptism, and perhaps place one or two informed church members to sit with the children and help them find their place in the books which may be used. Observers attending Christian services are still something of a novelty and congregations need to be prepared so that they can take it in their stride. They might even provide some refreshments. Children need to be reminded of the courtesies and assured that they may choose whether or not to sing hymns.

Even if the visit is, as most will be, to an empty building, it is always important for the teacher to make a preparatory visit, in order to be informed not only about the important aspects related to any visit, such as toilets and parking facilities, but also about the geography of the church and any peculiarities – brasses, war memorials, baptistries or wall-paintings. Never forget that churches can be cold even in the middle of summer!

Few churches can or should be covered in their totality in one visit, but children should be given time to orientate themselves and make themselves at ease if they have never before been to a church.

Think about your topic – perhaps baptism, or the church as the focus of the community – and concentrate on things which are relevant to it. Next time it might be the eucharist, and attention will focus on the altar/communion table, perhaps with the clergy-person showing the artefacts used, putting on vestments and simulating a eucharist. Another time, around Easter, the emphasis might be on the church preparing for Easter. Will crosses be covered? What colours will be used for the altar cloth? Will there be an Easter garden to look at? There is much to be said for primary schools, especially, establishing educational links with one or two places of worship and cultivating the friendship of their members and ministers. Choice depends on such factors as geographical convenience and friendliness, as much as religious considerations.

Visitors

These will be easily available if sound links have been established with local religious communities. These people, however, are resources. The teacher is the professional and must gently inform even the most authoritarian vicar of the purpose of the visit. On the rare occasions when things go wrong it is usually because of lack of briefing. Members of the clergy asked to 'come and speak to the children' can only fall back on their own experience as ministers of the Gospel. If the invitation is to talk about a day in their working life, what Easter means to them, why they decided to be ordained, or the challenge of taking a funeral, you should get something succinct and in keeping with the course. A preliminary meeting with a visitor can be helpful. You may not be able to communicate the objective approach to study that you have been helping your class to acquire, but you should be able to remove some of the threat which the visitor is feeling. Don't forget expenses and the offer of transport.

Members of faiths can bring authenticity and personal experience into the classroom in a way that teachers cannot, even if they think it to be appropriate. Visitors may also bring credibility – like the Indian Christian nun who eventually convinced a group of students that caste and arranged marriages are a feature of Indian Christianity (they had refused to believe their tutor!) Maybe a Roman Catholic could tell the class about a visit to Lourdes to enhance your study of pilgrimage, or someone could explain what prayer means to them.

Simulations

We often come across teachers who have simulated a Passover seder but eucharists are dealt with less frequently. If you are among those who hesitate to simulate holy communion, having simulated a rite in another religion, we would ask you to consider your reasons. Islamic prayer, Hindu puja, the Sabbath meal (for which Jews hoarded their meagre supplies of bread in the concentration camps) are no less sacred than the eucharist. They are all means through which God's sustaining presence or grace is believed to reach the believer. Is the barrier ignorance, or fear that some of the children may know more? Is it concern about parental reaction? We need to think through our objections and personal reactions. If we can accept that we are partners with our children in the learning experience, some of our anxieties may evaporate.

A simple simulation at Key Stage 1 or Key Stage 2 would be to cover a table with a white cloth, place two candles, a bread roll and a chalice of juice on it and tell the children that this is similar to what they might see if they went to church one Sunday morning. Add to it a simplified version of the story of the meal which Jesus shared with his friends. The emphasis would be upon friendship and the place of food in expressing it. The preliminary work leading up to the simulation would have been on family parties, picnics, class celebrations – the exploration of things which we do to demonstrate and strengthen our relationships. The Christian family meal's setting could be in a topic on Easter, worship or food, or it could be free-standing.

It is at Key Stage 3 and even more at Key Stage 4 that the words 'This is my body...This is my blood' would be introduced and the full significance of the Christian celebration studied. At this point the use of video would help.

There are clergy who are now accustomed to simulating eucharists for schools and enjoy it. They have overcome the difficulties of distancing and have come to terms with the issues involved. One of them might be invited to visit the class or might invite the class to visit the church, so that a simulation can be held with vestments, altar or communion table.

At Key Stage 4 the reasons for the ceremonial, the role of priest in some traditions, the concepts of sacred and secular could be developed from the simulation in such a way that the 'officiant' might look forward to the next visit. We have even heard of a Key Stage 4 PSE topic on marriage involving a range of subjects and ending with a reception after the church wedding. Here it was essential to have clergy support.

It is absolutely essential to keep parents fully informed about visits to a church for a eucharistic simulation. The letter should be as explanatory as possible and could include an invitation to join the class.

Poems, music and art

Hymns, religious poetry and prayers, and the visual arts should certainly be studied, and some hymns and poems might be learned. All are ways in which women and men through the ages have attempted to express the meaning which religion has for them and to share their experiences with others. Perhaps we have neglected this dimension too often in RE. But what of composing them? We would suggest that this might be one of the activities which children might like to undertake out of a range of possibilities. In a class where good relationships have been established they should feel comfortable and confident enough to do this without threat of mockery or other forms of bullying, but if they are not believers, of course, they may not wish to do so.

Imaginative and creative writing

Our colleagues in other disciplines might distinguish carefully between these. We would be interested in encouraging writing, which many children enjoy, to be more than retelling a story in one's own words. What did a child at the Hinton St Mary villa in Dorset think when he saw the mosaicists laying a floor with the face of Jesus, someone he may never have heard of, in the centre? Reconstruct the conversation he may have had with the designer or his parents. Or what of St Patrick when he, a young Christian, found himself a slave in a non-Christian land? (We have avoided 'pagan', or words like 'heathen' or 'superstition'. They usually carry pejorative meaning which we would not like to have attached to our cherished beliefs.)

Or the writing task might be an imaginative reflection upon a first communion, or on going on a pilgrimage to Lourdes.

Slides, photographs, videos and making videos

There are still teachers who assume knowledge of what the inside of a church looks like, or who rely on black and white pictures in textbooks. Colour photographs can now be converted into good quality OHPs fairly inexpensively. Photographs might be taken by pupils on a visit to a place of religious interest, turned into OHPs and used in follow-up lessons. Even better is the making of videos. Field studies in the sciences or history should not have all the fun and prestige of using camcorders. There are questions to be discussed about what to record, and the analysis of the material back in the classroom. Pupils might spend some time in the church deciding what they should photograph and from what angle. The preparation and follow-up should ensure doing more than taking pretty pictures. Such work can be part of a pupil's assessment from Key Stage 2 onwards. 'Describe some of the things found in a church' might ask for written or oral recollection but 'Explain how they are used' could be answered by visual images, backed up by spoken commentary.

Of course permissions may have to be obtained, especially in cathedrals or museums.

Drama

This is perhaps to be classed with the study or composition of poems or works of art mentioned above, as key ways of exploring religious ideas and practices. Watching a play which explores a religious theme – for example, a passion play – may be possible, but we are more interested in the use of drama to explore or develop understanding than in presentations for other reasons. The nativity play is seldom a religious education activity – exploration, empathy and understanding are missing from an activity which is usually aimed at impressing parents, governors and other visitors. It may seem to be religious but it is not RE as we envisage it. It could be, however, if it is the product of research and reflection and attempts to reach some of the great issues which the nativity stories deal with (see pages 107–13).

Discussions, brainstorming, buzz sessions

Informed explorations of religious ideas and actions should be encouraged and responses carefully considered. A feature of religious studies is that there are often several acceptable answers, and when working with children we have often been made to reconsider a view which we have accepted and taught for many years. We have drawn attention to a variety of interpretations in discussing parables (see pages 35–6). The four Gospels are evidence of diversity and the Church has never dared to say which one of several theories explaining the meaning of Jesus' death is the correct one. Discussion does demand input, however. Without stimulus nothing very lively is likely to happen. If, for example, the question of whether it is better for clergy to be married or not is to be discussed, there is a need to assemble as much material as possible on the subject. What is the biblical evidence? Has celibacy always been the rule? Why does the rule of celibacy exist? Why do some churches uphold it? Why do others reject it and almost accept that it is preferable for a minister to be married? A similar approach can be taken to Christian views on other contemporary matters: vegetarianism, pacifism, divorce, sexual relations outside marriage, homosexuality, abortion, choosing the sex of a baby, and many others. We would not encourage debates on these subjects – they are often based on inadequate information, encourage pupils to take sides prematurely and place attention on opinion rather than knowledge and understanding. And, of course, if the study is of Christian views, how many pupils have a right to express a position? It is much better to concentrate on understanding what different views there are and why Christians hold a variety of positions on many aspects of values.

Information-gathering

This is, as we have seen, a prerequisite for discussion. It is as important in RE as it is in History or scientific field study. It can vary from gathering information about the history of a local church to standing outside a supermarket asking shoppers what happened on Good Friday and Easter Day, or taking a census of religion in the catchment area of the school (if these exercises are considered appropriate). Church notice boards often carry information which can be used in RE lessons. In a middle school or Year 5 of a primary school, where one teacher is responsible for the humanities area of the curriculum, it should be possible to combine History and RE. The information may be identical but in RE we would be concentrating upon purpose, meaning, such issues as why the church was built and why people went there Sunday upon Sunday, and even why Sunday is the significant day – something which the historian might ignore, having a different agenda.

Oral religious history

This is as important as any other method of learning. 'Whit walks' of long ago or grandma describing her wedding or a family christening can breathe life into something which might otherwise be commonplace, especially if she brings a christening robe or wedding photographs. It may stimulate children to go home and ask about similar events in the stories of their own families. Displays in the hall about the local church or a baptism might attract the attention of visitors on a parents' day or evening when RE would otherwise pass unnoticed.

There are also popular religious beliefs to be uncovered. What beliefs are there about baptism? Is it still regarded as unlucky to take children out if they have not first been to church? How many grooms or best men are now expected to throw money for children to scramble for at weddings? There is often the folk-religion world of great-grandparents waiting to be explored.

Devising their own religious rites

This can be a way of discovering what has been learned and understood about the need for and purpose of rituals. Some very sensitive work has been done by an excellent teacher who explored the consequences of death on a desert island with her class. They produced a drama, beginning with the accident which caused death, examining the mourning of the community, and creating a ritual for disposing of the body. It was a school in which links with the home that the children came from were very close and parents were very involved with the performance. The children eventually wanted to produce the drama to share with the school and visitors. Some Christians think that to learn about existing rites is enough, but this can be a way of discovering whether their meaning has been understood.

Cookery

This is a very appropriate experience to organize at Key Stage 1 and Key Stage 2. Food, from hot cross buns to mince-pies, pancakes and simnel cakes, is as important in the Christian tradition as in any other. At Key Stage 1 and Key Stage 2, invite some parents to come in and help the class to prepare foods for festivals in manageable groups of six or eight (no larger). Then find out their significance. Painting hard boiled eggs has its place in RE, if the symbolism of the egg is the real focus of the lesson.

Model-making

Observational skills are often best developed when there is a practical reason acting as a stimulus. Learning about scale in Mathematics could well result in making a scale model of the church, which could be displayed in school and then given to the local Christian community. Similarly, an Easter garden might be created in the school hall before Easter. A vicar with vestments and a choir in procession, are just some of the other models that could be made. It might be possible to show an infant or believer's baptism with scale models, and Quakers sitting meditatively in a Friends' Meeting House. John Wesley preached in many church yards. This scene might be portrayed by models in a project combining with History to find the correct period dress.

Displays

Photographs, paintings, personal reflections, newspaper cuttings etc. are good ways of presenting material, which might range from studies of Jesus to Christian action in the community. If they can be assembled in the hall or corridor they can be used as the means of getting children in different classes to exchange ideas, opinions and information.

Collages are ways of achieving a similar result with greater emphasis upon aesthetics and expressionism.

Exhibitions, as part of a local religious event or for parents' evenings, can give purpose to pupil research.

Making greetings cards can be more than a scissors-and-paste activity one wet Friday afternoon. The process of selection, the exploration and use of symbolism, and the choice of an appropriate biblical verse, are ways of combining craft activity with thinking about religious significance.

Assemblies or acts of worship can provide opportunities for a class to share its work with other school groups. This provides the class with aims and encourages the development of communication skills, as well as opportunities for discussion in the playground or on the way home afterwards. This works particularly well at Key Stage 2 and Key Stage 3 but there are plenty of possibilities at Key Stage 4 and beyond.

Children like **making board games**. These could be based on a visit to Lourdes or being an observer during Holy Week; they could be used to check on information acquired during a topic, or could involve pictures of Christmas customs to be identified and explained. The makers of the game need to do some research and the other players need to demonstrate knowledge. Spiritual pursuits might be an alternative to trivial pursuits!

This is only a selection of possibilities, intended to suggest that RE can be a vehicle for active learning as much as any other subject on the curriculum, and should be. But activities can take time. They should not be allowed to take the place of actually studying beliefs and values.

Using children as resources

It is a great and natural temptation to use the Hindu or Christian child as a resource. Religion has to do with human beings and RE can be most successful when it is humanized. So believers in the classroom present us with a wonderful opportunity to bring religion to life.

Do you remember occasions when we were picked out in class? 'Mary's dad's a newsagent. She can tell us how many different dailies there are', or 'Michael's mum's a dentist. He can tell us how many teeth an adult should have'. In matters religious we are likely to ask a child who goes to church questions which would cause many Christians to feel threatened if they were asked on the way out of church. The child's knowledge might be slight, or they may wish to keep their beliefs and practices private.

We must also remember that the difference between being a believer and being a teacher or student is that the believer is doing things which are so much part of his or her life that they do not need explanation. People who are accustomed to kneel when praying probably do not reflect on the reason for doing so until they find out that Jews stand to pray in a synagogue or, perhaps, go to a church where the congregation sits to sing hymns and stands for prayer, as in Germany, for example. Most children do what they do because that is how they are being brought up. Often they cannot be expected to provide us with any better explanations for their actions than that.

Children may be used as resources so long as we have quietly, in private, discovered their willingness and negotiated the extent of their participation. 'We're going to the church that I think you go to, Robert, the one in Manvers Street, to look at the place where people get baptized. Would you like to tell us about it when we get there?' gives Robert a chance to opt in or out, and the question is put in language he can understand. 'Baptistry' and 'Baptist' are words which may not yet be part of his vocabulary. He may decide against involvement but start to chip in when he feels secure in the church he attends. 'That's where I sit with my mum and dad', he might say. Let him feel comfortable and contribute what he can and will.

A child may know the clergyman as 'Father Bill' instead of priest or vicar, so a blank look would greet the name of Father Harland. We must try to operate at the children's own level of religious practice. It is the practices that they may be best able to help us with, especially if they are of primary age. Their religion is something they do.

Children come from homes that can be rich in resources of all kinds – miners' lamps, war medals, Victorian christening robes and family Bibles – as well as relatives who may be willing to come to school. Once interest has been aroused and confidence won, the human resources and artefacts of a community can be at your disposal, but it must never be forgotten that you are the professional teacher.

All this having been said, there is one extremely important reason which still remains to be explained for involving the children, their parents and the community in what we do: self-esteem. Teachers are often tempted to lose their professional self-respect because society does not appear to value them. Perhaps they are consequently in a better position than most to appreciate the needs of others for self-respect. The child whose culture is demonstrated to be of value because it is taught about in the school, or the ministers who are better known in the community by being welcomed into the school, are likely to be better persons for the experience. Consequently the school must benefit, too. At the merely practical level, many teachers can speak of the improvement on academic attainment in all subjects and in discipline that has resulted from such a recognition of children's beliefs, and of positive developments in relationships with the community.

Skills, attitudes and concepts

Few skills and attitudes, if any, are peculiar to Religious Education. They can be found in most other areas of the humanities. Concepts, however, tend to be subject-specific. Concepts related to rituals, worship or God, for example, belong to the study of religions, not to History or Literature, and are essential aspects of Religious Education.

Whatever subjects we are teaching we should be seeking to deal with at least one concept and probably several skills and attitudes, if children are to be religiously educated. We might subject our teaching to the scrutiny of the list in the following box. (No correspondence is intended between the two lists.)

Skills and/or attitudes	Concepts
willingness to see and listen without wishing to make judgements	faith and belief
	worship
readiness to share the experiences and ideas of others	prayer
guided imagination	meditation
expression of thoughts and feelings	meaning
curiosity and skills of investigation	ritual
use of religious language	religion
evaluation of evidence	ethics/morality
respect for oneself and others	commitment
promotion of positive attitudes towards understanding beliefs and values	myth
	what it means to belong to a faith community

Further reading

For the teacher

An Introduction to the use of Artefacts in RE, Vida Barnett, Articles of Faith.*
Religious Artefacts in the Classroom, P Gateshill and J Thompson, Hodder and
Stoughton, 1992.*

For the classroom

Christian Artefacts Pack, Vida Barnett, Articles of Faith.* This takes the form of
photocopiable worksheets.

*These and a considerable range of artefacts can be obtained from Articles of
Faith. The address is given in Appendix 2.

7 The Bible

The 1947 Agreed Syllabus of Religious Instruction of the West Riding of Yorkshire defined the aim of its primary school syllabus as being 'to present the revelation of God given in the Bible'. The place of the Bible in Religious Education is an emotive subject. Even today, especially in primary schools, Bible stories constitute the major part of an RE syllabus.

The view of this book is that children in this country are not properly educated until they understand the nature and use of the Bible and its place in Christianity. We would argue, however, that, as with the teaching of Christianity in general, we are calling for something new, rather than assuming a continuity of present practice.

We would challenge the assumption that to give children a 'diet' of Bible stories automatically helps them to understand the Bible itself. Perhaps even more importantly, we feel that it is an insult to the sacred text of millions of believers if it is presented to children out of context, alongside all the many other 'stories' they learn at school. Not only does this devalue the nature of the biblical material; the 'hidden agenda' sensed by the children often results in distrust or even hostility, rather than fascination or respect. This problem is not helped by attempts in primary schools to make Bible stories more 'relevant' by including them in a topic, just because they seem to refer, in some way, to the subject being explored. This can lead to terrible distortions of the stories themselves – such as the account of the feeding of the five thousand in a project on 'Litter'. We have even encountered the story of the flight into Egypt in a topic on 'Flight'! It is difficult to imagine such poor educational practice being tolerated in any other area of the curriculum. In the same way, we would argue that secondary school pupils are not helped to understand the nature of the Bible by forcing tenuous links between biblical material, out of context, and the discussion of some modern social issue.

We do, however, believe that there is a way in which the Bible can be taught which encourages pupils to respect it but which does not presuppose a particular belief for them or for their teacher. We believe that the golden rule for teaching about the Bible is always to look at biblical material in the context of the believing community which produced it and now treasure it as scripture. By following this rule we believe that all the potential problems mentioned above can be avoided.

1 The biblical material is not devalued; it is always presented as something sacred to a particular group of people.

2 The integrity of the pupils is being respected because they are not automatically being asked to believe the claims of the Bible, but they are being asked to *respect* it because of its importance to millions of Christians.

3 This approach makes the use of biblical material in the classroom much easier for Christian and non-Christian teachers. The source of authority for this material now lies not with the teacher, but with the community. Inevitable questions such as 'But is it true?' 'Did it happen?' can be answered without the teacher having to make a personal commitment, or declare a lack of it. The answer is: 'Well, let's look at the way Christians tell and understand this story / remember this festival / follow this teaching – what can we learn about the truth of this for them?'

4 This approach also reflects an understanding of the biblical material which has emerged as a result of the modern scholarship developed over the last 200 years. This biblical analysis has developed within Christianity. It has greatly influenced the Christian approaches to the Bible in modern western Christianity that lie behind the culture of this country. There are, of course, some Christians who do not accept this approach and do not feel a need to. For many it is simply not an issue. Every minister training for the mainstream Christian denominations of this country, however, is introduced to these methods of critical study.

We are not suggesting that these methods themselves should be introduced to the pupils until Key Stages 4 and above (even then, it must be made clear that not all Christians agree with them). Nor are we suggesting that every teacher attempting RE must be conversant with what scholars term Source, Form and Redaction Criticism of the Bible! We do, however, hope to show that a basic understanding of its general approach can be understood and applied to every Key Stage level. In fact, we would argue that the main message of the modern methods of biblical study is the same as our golden rule – *that biblical material should be understood as the product of a believing community who then transmitted it until it came to be regarded as Scripture.*

Modern methods of studying the Bible

This approach is often described as Biblical Criticism, and this can cause much misunderstanding. In this context, criticism does not mean 'finding fault with' but is being used in the technical sense of 'making judgements from an informed position'. As already stated, these methods of study have not been developed by those who wish to devalue the Bible. On the contrary, the scholars were and are Christians who want to understand more fully the nature and purpose of biblical material. The methods of study were developed in the 19th century as a result of the changed perceptions in the west demonstrated through the Renaissance, Reformation and Enlightenment, but also as a response to the negative effects of the 'Age of Reason' on an understanding of the Bible as 'truth'. For many Christians today, the scholars' explanation of biblical material are of great benefit to their faith. They allow them to relate to the expressions of religious experience of believers thousands of years ago and find truth in them, regardless of whether they share their assumptions that the world was flat, or that epilepsy was caused by evil spirits. For them, the ability to understand the Bible as a complex record of the quest of a community to understand God's message, is liberating. It reveals the Bible as the inspired word of God – regardless of the confusions, contradictions and difficulties they find there.

The first attempts to apply critical methods of study to the Bible were made in investigations into the first five books of the Old Testament, known as the Pentateuch, and on the first three Gospels in the New Testament, known as the Synoptic Gospels. A brief survey of the ways in which modern scholarship effected an understanding of this material will give some insight into the methods involved. It will also, we hope, allow teachers to see how the results of those methods can help them present Bible stories in the classroom.

The Pentateuch

The traditional belief about the first five books of the Bible is that they were written by Moses. When scholars studied the material carefully, however, they came to the conclusion that the many variations, repetitions and inconsistencies there indicated that it could not have been written by any one author, let alone Moses. They also discovered that some of the material reflected a time much much later than that of Moses.

A good example of the issues and questions raised by a careful analysis of biblical material is given when we look at Genesis chapters 1 and 2. The scholars realized that here we have not one but *two* versions of the Creation. At Genesis chapter 2 verse 4, one version ends and another begins. An important clue to the fact that there are two different accounts is the use of different names for God in each one. This is reflected in the English translation here by the phrase 'God' in one version and 'Lord God' in the other.

Here are the two accounts.

Genesis 1:1–2:4

1 'In the beginning God created the heavens and the earth. [2]The earth was without form and void, and darkness was upon the face of the deep; and the Spirit of God was moving over the face of the waters. [3]And God said,

"Let there be light"; and there was light. [4]And God saw that the light was good; and God separated the light from the darkness. [5]God called the light Day, and the darkness he called Night. And there was evening and there was morning, one day. [6]And God said, "Let there be a firmament in the midst of the waters, and let it separate the waters from the waters." [7]And God made the firmament and separated the waters which were under the firmament from the waters which were above the firmament. And it was so. [8]And God called the firmament Heaven. And there was evening and there was morning, a second day. [9]And God said, "Let the waters under the heavens be gathered together into one place, and let the dry land appear." And it was so. [10]God called the dry land Earth, and the waters that were gathered together he called Seas. And God saw that it was good. [11]And God said, "Let the earth put forth vegetation, plants yielding seed, and fruit trees bearing fruit in which is their seed, each according to its kind, upon the earth." And it was so. [12]The earth brought forth vegetation, plants yielding seed according to their own kinds, and trees bearing fruit in which is their seed, each according to its own kind. And God saw that it was good. [13]And there was evening and there was morning, a third day. [14]And God said, "Let there be lights in the firmament of the heavens to separate the day from the night; and let them be for signs and for seasons and for days and years, [15]and let them be lights in the firmament of the heavens to give light upon the earth." And it was so. [16]And God made the two great lights, the greater light to rule the day, and the lesser light to rule the night; he made the stars also. [17]And God set them in the firmament of the heavens to give light upon the earth, [18]to rule over the day and over the night, and to separate the light from the darkness. And God saw that it was good. [19]And there was evening and there was morning, a fourth day. [20]And God said, "Let the waters bring forth swarms of living creatures, and let birds fly above the earth across the firmament of the heavens." [21]So God created the great sea monsters and every living creature that moves, with which the waters swarm, according to their kinds, and every winged bird according to its kind. And God saw that it was good. [22]And God blessed them, saying, "Be fruitful and multiply and fill the waters in the seas, and let birds multiply on the earth." [23]And there was evening and there was morning, a fifth day. [24]And God said, "Let the earth bring forth living creatures according to their kinds: cattle and creeping things and beasts of the earth according to their kinds." And it was so. [25]And God made the beasts of the earth according to their kinds and the cattle according to their kinds, and everything that creeps upon the ground according to its kind. And God saw that it was good. [26]Then God said, "Let us make man in our image, after our likeness; and let them have dominion over the fish of the sea, and over the birds of the air, and over the cattle, and over all the earth, and over every creeping thing that creeps upon the earth." [27]So God created man in his own image, in the image of God he created him; male and female he created them. [28]And God blessed them, and God said to them, "Be fruitful and multiply, and fill the earth and subdue it; and have dominion over the fish of the sea and over the birds of the air and over every living thing that moves upon the earth." [29]And God said, "Behold, I have given you every plant yielding seed which is upon the face of all the earth, and every tree with seed in its fruit; you shall have them for food. [30]And to every beast of the earth, and to every bird of the air, and to everything that creeps on the earth, everything that has the breath of life, I have given every green plant for food." And it was so. [31]And God saw everything that he had made, and behold, it was very good. And there was evening and there was morning, a sixth day.

2 Thus the heavens and the earth were finished, and all the host of them. [2]And on the seventh day God finished his work which he had done, and he rested on the seventh day from all his work which he had done. [3]So God blessed the seventh day and hallowed it, because on it God rested from all his work which he had done in creation. [4]These are the generations of the heavens and the earth when they were created.'

Genesis 2:4–25

'In the day that the LORD God made the earth and the heavens, [5]when no plant of the field was yet in the earth and no herb of the field had yet sprung up – for the LORD God had not caused it to rain upon the earth, and there was no man to till the ground; [6]but a mist went up from the earth and watered the whole face of the ground – [7]then the LORD God formed man of dust from the ground, and breathed into his nostrils the breath of life; and man became a living being. [8]And the LORD God planted a garden in Eden, in the east; and there he put the man whom he had formed. [9]And out of the ground the LORD God made to grow every tree that is pleasant to the sight and good for food, the tree of life also in the midst of the garden, and the tree of the knowledge of good and evil. [10]A river flowed out of Eden to water the garden, and there it divided and became four rivers. [11]The name of the first is Pishon; it is the one which flows around the whole land of Hav'ilah, where there is gold; [12]and the gold of that land is good; bdellium and onyx stone are there. [13]The name of the second river is Gihon; it is the one which flows around the whole land of Cush. [14]And the name of the third river is Tigris, which flows east of Assyria. And the fourth river is the Eu-phra'tes. [15]The LORD God took the man and put him in the garden of Eden to till it and keep it. [16]And the LORD God commanded the man, saying, "You may freely eat of every tree of the garden; [17]but of the tree of the knowledge of good and evil you shall not eat, for in the day that you eat of it you shall die."

¹⁸Then the LORD God said, "It is not good that the man should be alone; I will make him a helper fit for him." ¹⁹So out of the ground the LORD God formed every beast of the field and every bird of the air, and brought them to the man to see what he would call them; and whatever the man called every living creature, that was its name. ²⁰The man gave names to all cattle, and to the birds of the air, and to every beast of the field; but for the man there was not found a helper fit for him. ²¹So the LORD God caused a deep sleep to fall upon the man, and while he slept took one of his ribs and closed up its place with flesh; ²²and the rib which the LORD God had taken from the man he made into a woman and brought her to the man. ²³Then the man said, "This at last is bone of my bones and flesh of my flesh; she shall be called Woman, because she was taken out of Man." ²⁴Therefore a man leaves his father and his mother and cleaves to his wife, and they become one flesh. ²⁵And the man and his wife were both naked, and were not ashamed.'

When both accounts are seen in this way, we can appreciate the differences in the story of how the world began. In the first account, humans are made at the end of the creative process, which takes seven days. In the second version the male human is made first and the rest of creation is made around him until eventually the female human is made to be his partner. It is important to note, however, that although the stories are different, the religious message is the same – that humans are the 'pinnacle' of God's creation and have a special responsibility to look after the world. Likewise, the stories differ when describing the special creation of human beings. Genesis 1:27 describes humans as being 'male and female in the image of God', and Genesis 2:7 offers the vivid and graphic account of God moulding the male human from clay and breathing into him. Again, the stories are different but the theological message is the same – that humans have a unique relationship with God and that God can best be understood by looking at human qualities and relationships. These are sophisticated ideas which Christians today would still claim to be true. These stories, therefore, also highlight the fact that the meaning of a biblical account is found not by asking the question 'Did it happen?' but by asking 'Why was this story told and what did it mean to those who told it?'

As a result of this kind of analysis a theory was presented which is now accepted as the basis for an informed understanding of the nature and purpose of the writings found in the Pentateuch. What we now read in the first five books of the Bible is a compilation of four different accounts of Israel's early history, produced over a period of about 500 years. The scholars who 'discovered' these four accounts used different letters to distinguish them: J, E, P and D.

'J' refers to an account of the sacred history of the formation of Israel written in the Southern Kingdom about 1,000 years BCE. This was during the time of

David or Solomon. The account was written to show how 12 nomadic tribes had come together to form one powerful nation under a monarchy. The history is presented to demonstrate how God has guided the formation of Israel and made them God's people.

'E' is a very similar sacred history, written a little later in the Northern Kingdom. It is distinguished from 'J' by its use of a different name for God.

'D' was a new interpretation of the sacred history of Israel, written in response to the crisis caused by the invasion of the Northern Kingdom by a foreign empire in 721BCE. This was interpreted as a punishment for the people's failure to keep the laws that God had given them and to worship God alone.

'P' was the final account of Israel's early history, written about 500 years after the first. This time the need to reflect on Israel's past was brought about by an even greater disaster. The remainder of Israel had been conquered by a new enemy, the Babylonian empire. Jerusalem had been taken, the Temple destroyed, the King removed and most of the people carried off into exile. In the face of this terrible crisis, the priests had to show that the special relationship between God and Israel still existed and that God was the powerful creator of the world who had punished Israel in order to bring her back to him.

Shortly after the writing of this last version, all four accounts were combined and made into the five books of the Law, which became the sacred scripture of Israel. An understanding of how these biblical books came about helps to underline the fact that this material should not be treated as 'history' as we understand it today, but as a faith statement about the special relationship between God and Israel – as revealed in God's acts in history.

In the light of this understanding, we can return to the Creation stories and realize that chapter 1 is from the 'P' source, and chapter 2 from the 'J'. Chapter 1 was therefore written about 500 years after chapter 2. It was re-interpreting the story as a response to the great upheavals that Israel was going through. The magnificent picture of God as Creator of the Universe helped to reassure the exiled Israelites that their Yahweh was the true God, not the Babylonian gods. There are, therefore, echoes in this story of the Babylonian creation epic. The inclusion of a seven-day process of creation, with God resting on the seventh day, reflects the increased importance of the Sabbath. In the absence of the Temple, those elements of the religion which affirmed a sense of identity, such as the keeping of the Sabbath and food laws and circumcision, took on a new significance. The basic theology, however, is just the same as the story written 500 years earlier.

The Synoptic Gospels

When the scholars' attention turned to the Gospels, they found that they were faced with similar questions when trying to understand the material they read. They found that it was possible to look at the first three Gospels alongside one another and appreciate that they have a great deal of material in common. Sometimes passages appear in all three Gospels, word for word the same; sometimes they are very similar, but with slight variations. Sometimes a passage will appear in only two of the Gospels, sometimes in only one. Presenting the material of the Gospels in this way is called providing a synopsis – a word which comes from the Greek for 'looking at something together'. For this reason Matthew, Mark and Luke are known as the Synoptic Gospels. The Gospel of John does not fit into this pattern, and therefore stands separately.

We can see an example of the questions facing the scholars if we look at the three versions of the baptism of Jesus in Matthew, Mark and Luke.

Matthew 3:13–17

'[13]Then Jesus came from Galilee to the Jordan to John, to be baptized by him. [14]John would have prevented him, saying, "I need to be baptized by you, and do you come to me?" [15]But Jesus answered him, "Let it be so now; for thus it is fitting for us to fulfil all righteousness." Then he consented. [16]And when Jesus was baptized, he went up immediately from the water, and behold, the heavens were opened and he saw the Spirit of God descending like a dove, and alighting on him; [17]and lo, a voice from heaven, saying, "This is my beloved Son, with whom I am well pleased."'

Mark 1:9–11

'[9]In those days Jesus came from Nazareth of Galilee and was baptized by John in the Jordan. [10]And when he came up out of the water, immediately he saw the heavens opened and the Spirit descending upon him like a dove; [11]and a voice came from heaven, "Thou art my beloved Son; with thee I am well pleased."'

Luke 3:21–2

'[21]Now when all the people were baptized, and when Jesus also had been baptized and was praying, the heaven was opened, [22]and the Holy Spirit descended upon him in bodily form, as a dove, and a voice came from heaven, "Thou art my beloved Son; with thee I am well pleased."'

When we look at the material in this way we can see that the accounts are very similar – and yet there are significant differences. For instance, Matthew's account includes some conversation between Jesus and John which is not recorded elsewhere. It also records the words from heaven in a slightly different form.

This is just one small example of the many similarities and differences in the Gospel material which presented so many questions for the scholars. One very important question became: what exactly *is* a Gospel?

What is a Gospel?

The traditional belief about the Gospels of Matthew, Mark and Luke is that they are biographies of Jesus, written from eye-witness accounts. The result of careful analysis showed that this was a misunderstanding of their nature and purpose. A breakthrough in attempts to make sense of the Gospels came when scholars realized that, contrary to Church tradition, Mark, not Matthew, was written first – and that Luke and Matthew used Mark as a written source. This made sense of the literary relationship between the three works. Mark was the 'proto-type' which provided the structure for the others to follow. It was not an eye-witness account, but the product of a faith community. The word 'gospel' means 'a good proclamation' or 'good news' as some Christians say. The first verse of Mark's Gospel states its purpose clearly: 'The beginning of the gospel of Jesus Christ, the Son of God'. This is a very clear statement of faith, and everything that follows is written to confirm that statement. There is a remarkable lack of interest in biographical detail. We discover very little about the personal life of Jesus of Nazareth. Mark's Gospel tells us nothing at all about his life before his mission began. We hear about his family only in passing. Most of the Gospel covers the last few days of Jesus' life. The concern of all the stories found in the Gospels is not to give biographical information but to show that Jesus is the Christ, or Messiah, and the son of God. Like the Pentateuch, the Gospels are not concerned to present 'history' in the way that we understand it, but with showing how God is acting in history.

The Gospels of Matthew and Luke use some of the stories found in Mark, often interpreting them to explain them in a new way. In addition, they include material fom another source, known as 'Q', and stories which are unique to them (see Chapter 11 on Christmas).

If we return to the accounts of the Baptism, we see that Matthew and Luke have used Mark's account and sometimes adapted it. The original story is there not for 'historical interest', but because it shows Jesus as the Messiah and son of God. In Mark's account, this is a personal experience: we are told that Jesus sees the heavens open and hears the words. It is an important theme in Mark's Gospel that Jesus is the 'hidden' Messiah. The reader is shown Jesus' true nature from the start, but the narrative tells that Jesus' contemporaries did not recognize him as the Messiah. Even the disciples are shown as failing to understand Jesus' mission until after the resurrection.

In Matthew, however, this event becomes a public one. The heavens are opened and the words declare to the crowd: 'This is my son.' Scholars believe that the Gospel of Matthew was written when the early Church was trying to establish itself and was engaged in debate with the rest of Judaism about the validity of their claim that Jesus was the Messiah. Matthew therefore emphasizes the divine confirmation of Jesus' mission. It would also seem that by the time this account is written, there was some difficulty for the Church in explaining why Jesus was baptized by John, if Jesus was greater than John and without need of forgiveness for sins. Matthew's version therefore inserts a conversation between them to explain this. In Luke's account, the story is worded so that it is not stated that John baptized Jesus.

This small example of the scholars' work illustrates their claim that the Gospels are not primarily biographies but proclamations of faith. It demonstrates the way in which we should appreciate these accounts as expressions of religious belief, and that their meaning lies not in historical research but in the living faith of the communities which preserved them, transmitted them, interpreted them and still cherish them as expressions of truth today.

Teaching suggestions

We can divide an approach to teaching about the Christian Bible into three areas:

1 the place of the Bible in Christianity
2 the nature of the Bible
3 content to be covered – Old Testament and New Testament.

1 The place of the Bible in Christianity

The Bible is very important as the sacred scripture, but it is Jesus who is central to Christianity. The Bible is about him (see Chapter 4 on the Christian world view). The Bible is believed to be inspired (this is understood in different ways) but nearly all Christians believe that the Bible provides an understanding of God's dealings with humanity.

• The reading of the Bible has a central place in Christian worship. Until relatively recently, individuals did not have access to Bibles; biblical texts were only transmitted through worship and teaching. This is still very much the case in many Christian traditions.

- Respect for the Bible is shown in different ways. In the western Protestant tradition the importance of the Bible is often shown by its constant use, by keeping a copy of the Bible nearby at all times. As a result the book itself can become very worn. One Christian poster proclaimed that 'if your Bible is falling apart, your life won't be.'
- In other traditions, however, for example the Eastern Orthodox, Christians show their respect by treating the actual book with great care. The Bible is brought into the service attended by a solemn procession. Worshippers show their reverence for the book by genuflecting, crossing themselves and ensuring that they do not turn their back on it. They would be horrified by the 'familiar' way in which Protestants treat the sacred text.

Key Stage 1

Arrange a visit to a local church which has a lectern and a large Bible for reading to those who sit in the pews. Discuss what this suggests about the specialness of this book for those people.

Ideally, this should take place before introducing the children to Bible stories. Then the stories can be put in that context: 'Remember the special book we saw in the church? Here is a smaller version of that book and some of the stories from it which are read in church.'

Children will meet Bible stories at festival times, especially Christmas (see Chapter 11). But again, they should be presented as stories told by Christians, or the people who go to church.

Key Stage 2

Pupils can learn more about the Bible in topics such as 'Writings', 'Books', 'Stories' or 'Communication'.

- They can learn about the ways in which Christians today show their respect for the Bible – e.g. the readings in church and ritual surrounding it and private devotion. They can learn about the careful transmission of the Bible in the past – scribes writing copies by hand, and the beautiful decorations of the illuminated manuscripts.
- Pupils need to see a variety of cultural expressions of biblical stories to show the relevance of the Bible to Christians throughout the world, and to avoid the view that Christianity, and even Jesus, is White, Anglo-Saxon and Protestant. (Resources for this are suggested at the end of the book.)

Key Stage 3

At this stage pupils can explore the place of the Bible and RE topics such as 'Holy Books' or 'Worship'. Here they can study in more detail the place of the Bible in Christian worship and private devotional reading. They can also learn more about the history of the translation of the Bible and of those who risked their lives to ensure the right to read the Bible: for example, the story of William Tyndale in this country and modern Christians in places like China.

Key Stage 4

By this stage pupils should have an awareness of the fact that different Christians understand the Bible as the 'word of God' in different ways – e.g. those who understand the truth of the Bible to be dependent on its historical and scientific accuracy, and those who apply modern methods of scholarship to make the Bible meaningful to their everyday lives.

The nature of the Bible

Key Stage 1

At this stage, pupils can be prepared for an understanding of the complex nature of the Bible by ensuring that the stories are always presented as 'special' to the people who tell them.

They can be introduced by words such as: 'some people tell this story to show that God helped people in the past'; or: 'Christians tell this story to show that Jesus was very special.'

The telling of stories can be used as a means of expressing truth.

Key Stage 2

Pupils can now be introduced to the Bible as a 'library' of books, rather than one book. This can be done most effectively by actually making the library of 66 books, using cereal boxes, for instance, and putting them on display. It is, however, best to avoid the traditional categories of literature. To use the term 'history', for instance, would be very confusing at this stage, as we have shown earlier in the chapter. Few books fall neatly into such categories as History or Poetry. It is best to concentrate on the fact that the Bible is a large collection of different books written at different times, by different people.

Key Stage 3

At this stage pupils *can* discover that the library of the Bible contains many different types of literature. Now is the time for them to appreciate the distinctive nature of 'sacred history' found in the Bible, and the distinctive nature of a 'gospel'. They can also see examples of poetry, letters and songs.

Key Stage 4

By this stage pupils can be introduced to the basic ideas of biblical scholarship. Pupils need not learn about the techniques themselves, but can appreciate the important implications of this approach – for instance, that the material should be understood as the expressions of religious belief of faith communities. They should also know that, for instance, there are two versions of the creation story and two versions of the birth narratives.

The content of the Bible

It could be argued that if we follow the golden rule and always present biblical material in the context of the faith community who transmit it, any material can be approached at any level; and that the depth to which it was explored would differ according to the pupils' ability. On the other hand, some ideas about the biblical stories are more difficult than others, and could perhaps be tackled later rather than sooner.

There are some general points about the content of the Bible that we need to consider. We need to be aware of the fascinating but often perplexing complexity of the biblical material and realize that some stories are not suitable for study in the classroom at all. The Christian tradition tends to have a 'canon within the canon' – in other words, some parts of the Bible are used much more than others. Some of the stories in the Old Testament, especially, raise all sorts of problems about sexual morality, the treatment of women and human rights. Such issues may be tackled in the sixth form – but, we would advise, not before then.

Miracles

Many teachers are worried about how they should tackle miracle stories in the classroom. The Bible includes many accounts of 'miraculous' happenings which usually prompt children to ask the questions which many teachers dread: 'Did it really happen?' 'Do *you* believe it, Miss?'

These are times when following the golden rule is especially important. The stories are told and often celebrated by Christians because their experience proves them to be true. The meaning and 'truth' of these accounts lies firmly with the believing community; the teacher, whether Christian or not, is not the source of authority here: the faith community is. Many teachers are tempted to provide some sort of 'rational' explanation for the miracles, in order to make them more acceptable in the classroom. This can apparently be done quite easily with some of the healing miracles, so that paralysis becomes the psychosomatic result of the sufferer's guilt, which is removed by Jesus' acceptance and forgiveness. Many teachers also know of the 'explanation' of the story of feeding the five thousand, where the little boy's generosity in giving up his humble meal prompts everyone else to share the food they were hiding for themselves, so that there is more than enough to go round. Such explanations may seem to make the stories more comfortable for some, but we would argue that this approach is not really appropriate. Those who use it often find that they run out of valid explanations when facing a story such as the calming of the storm and Jesus walking on the water but, more importantly, we would argue that such an approach is not true to the nature of these stories and their use in Christianity.

These stories were written by people who had a very different world view from nearly all the children in the classroom, and the meaning of the accounts needs to be understood, whether or not the children themselves want to accept that meaning for themselves. Etienne Charpentier, a Christian priest and scholar wrote that: 'a miracle is a sign only for believers. A present exchanged between friends is a present only because they are already friends; an object given to us in the street by an unknown person is not a sign but a question. If we are to recognize a particular fact as a miracle, we must already have faith. For the non-believer, a miracle is a question, and never a "proof".'

Many Christians believe that miracles happen today and that they are not something that only happened in the Bible. Some of them would also say that the way in which the miracles of Bible times are described reflects a way of understanding the world which is very different from today, even if they believe that the way of understanding God is the same. It is not the teacher's job to prove the miracles to their pupils, but to help them understand what they meant to the people who first wrote them, and to the people who tell those stories today.

We could look at two examples in order to see how we can try to understand miracles as signs to the believer.

The crossing of the Red Sea (Exodus chapter 14)

For many people, this story immediately conjures up Cecil B de Mille's epic and its graphic picture of the walls of water on either side of the fleeing Israelites. For others, it recalls the theory that the crossing was actually an estuary, where certain conditions made it possible for the Hebrews to cross, but proved fatal for the heavy armour and chariots of the Egyptians.

How should we understand this story?

First of all, we should be aware of the techniques of biblical analysis of the Pentateuch, and realize that there are in fact two versions of the story in Genesis 14. Unlike the creation accounts, they are not given one after another but intertwined. The familiar story of Moses raising his hand and forming walls of water in the 'P' account is shown in verses 16, 22, 26 and 28, for instance. There is also a 'J' account, which speaks of the Lord driving the sea back all night with a strong east wind and making the sea dry land for the Hebrews to cross. When the Egyptians followed, however, they found that the wheels of their chariots were 'clogged so that they drove heavily' and they panicked and fled. This account is in verses 21, 24 and 25. It is very tempting for 20th-century readers to say: 'Ah – so the 'J' account tells what really happened'. The biblical understanding is that *both* accounts tell what really happened. The 'J' account states that the Lord made the east wind blow all night. But the 'P' account is, if anything, more 'accurate' – because it emphasizes the fact that this remarkable escape was an example of God using divine power to act in history on behalf of his people. The 'truth' of this story for the Jewish tradition, for instance, is evident in the fact that they retell and re-live this miraculous escape every year in the festival of Pesach or Passover. A comparison of the 'P' account of the crossing of the Red Sea with the 'P' account of the creation will demonstrate that the writers used the same imagery of God separating the waters to form dry land in both stories.

The writers were showing that the same divine power which created the world saved the Israelites during the Exodus. This is the meaning of the story for Jews and Christians today – and this is what pupils need to understand.

Jesus calms the storm (Matthew 8:18–27, Mark 4:35–41, Luke 8:22–5)

This account may seem particularly difficult to deal with in the classroom. We need to appreciate, however, that all the 'miracle' stories in the Synoptic Gospels follow the same pattern and all, therefore, need to be understood as having the same purpose: showing the true nature of Jesus as Messiah and son of God. The pattern which they all follow is:

• an introduction which presents the situation
• a request for intervention which shows the faith of the people who ask, or the faith of those around them
• the intervention of Jesus
• the result
• the reaction of the spectators – fear, admiration or awe.

For the Gospel writers, Jesus' ability to overcome the evil powers which cause disturbances of nature reveals the same divine authority which overcomes the evil powers causing disease and disturbances in humans. The story immediately following this in Mark's Gospel is an account of Jesus healing a person possessed by many demons – and the pattern and purpose of both stories is the same. When looking at this story in the classroom, the questions the pupils need to ask are: 'Why did the early Christians tell this story? What does it tell us about their beliefs about Jesus?'

When considering this story with Key Stage 4 pupils, we would note that one of the reasons this story was so important to Christians at the time it was written was because they were suffering persecution and could identify with the cry of the disciples – 'Save, Lord, we are perishing'. This could lead to a discussion of what this story would therefore mean to Christians today.

Conclusion

Having considered some aspects of how to approach biblical material in the classroom, we conclude by making some suggestions as to the appropriate level at which specific content might be introduced.

Old Testament

Key Stage 1

It could be argued that it is not really necessary to deal with Old Testament material at this stage at all. If teachers want to introduce children to some simple examples, such as the story of David and Goliath or Joseph (whose coat was not actually 'multi-coloured' – see Genesis 37:3), they need to be presented as 'the stories that Christians tell' or part of the special book seen in the parish church.

Key Stage 2

At this stage, pupils could be introduced to material from Genesis and Exodus as stories of a faith community to show how God has created and protected them. The stories of Abraham, Isaac, Jacob and Joseph can be presented in this way, as can the story of Moses and the Exodus. Pupils could also read the creation accounts as stories told to show that the world was made and is protected by God. These stories might be examined within topics such as 'Communication', 'Books', 'Story' or 'Leaders'.

Key Stage 3

Any of the stories mentioned in Key Stage 2 could be left until this stage, or re-examined to be understood in more depth. The creation stories should certainly be considered at this stage. Older pupils at this stage could also be introduced to other Old Testament material to show the belief that God acts through historical events and speaks through chosen people. Presented in this way, they could learn about 'Judges' – Samson, for instance, and the prophets. They could learn about the exile and read some of the literature written at that time.

Key Stage 4

By this stage pupils should be aware of the very varied nature of biblical material. To help them appreciate this, they could look at the Psalms and 'wisdom literature'. They should also understand terms such as myth, legend, miracle and parable.

Further topics

At Key Stages 2/3 some stories about the discovery of Bible texts and the risks Christians have taken to translate and smuggle Bibles can be excitingly presented, so long as teachers remember that the importance of the Bible is the purpose of the study and not, primarily, history. The story of Mary Jones and her Bible is well known in Wales. Scotland and Ireland may have their own tales to explore. Wall paintings and stained glass windows provide some idea of which stories Christians consider most important. These could be read in modern translations and the help they give believers could be discussed.

Individual Christians might be willing to come to school to tell pupils what the Bible means to them and which passages they consider to be most important. At Key Stage 4 studies might be made of such denominations as the Free Church of Scotland, Plymouth Brethren or Seventh Day Adventists who centre their beliefs very firmly upon the Bible.

Issues

We have raised and discussed many issues in the course of this chapter. A discussion of the Bible in the classroom is fraught with issues. We hope, however, that we have provided a positive and helpful response to many of the questions surrounding this subject. There are, however, still some ideas to consider.

1 As we mentioned at the beginning of this chapter, teaching about the Bible is a very emotive issue. We have argued that teachers of Religious Education should know about the modern methods of biblical scholarship because it is educationally appropriate. We have also mentioned, however, that there are some Christians who do not accept the findings of this scholarship. These 'Bible Christians' constitute an important section of

the Christian tradition and their beliefs need to be respected. We are not saying that children should be taught that they must accept this scholarship itself. If teachers present the biblical material in the light of such scholarship – as the beliefs of a faith community – then there should be no reason for 'Bible Christians' to feel that their beliefs are being contradicted. We would also stress that all the scholarship we have discussed in this chapter comes from within Christianity. It is not an attempt of unbelievers to devalue the Bible; on the contrary, it is the work of Christians whose love and respect for the Bible has prompted them to understand it better. Nearly all Christians believe the Bible to be the inspired word of God, but the concept of 'inspiration' is understood in different ways. 'Bible Christians' feel that it is important to stress that 'inspired by God' means that the Bible is without error or contradiction of any kind. Many other Christians experience the Bible as conveying God's message to humanity, but do not feel that this conflicts with an acceptance of the results of biblical scholarship. To them, the people and communities who experience and interpret God's word are 'inspired', but their attempts to express this must inevitably be humanly fallible. Some Christians consider it idolatrous to attribute to the Bible the perfect qualities which are due only to God as revealed in Jesus.

2 We have to remember that much of the material found in the Christian Bible is also considered scripture by other faiths – Judaism and Islam. As mentioned above, the Christian Old Testament is almost identical to the Jewish Bible or Tenakh. It is just one of the fascinating complexities of the Christian scriptures that it has absorbed wholesale the scriptures of another faith. As on many other occasions, we have to be sure that in teaching about the Christian Bible we do not distort or deride the scriptures of the Jews. One important way to avoid this is to ensure that we do not use the term 'Old Testament' when discussing Judaism. For Jews the testament – covenant or agreement – is not 'old' or superseded; it is as relevant today as it was when given to Moses. Muslims believe that Jewish and Christian scriptures are a flawed and distorted version of the true message. Muslims do, however, share a respect for the prophets, among whom they include Jesus, and tell many stories about them. Teachers are often amazed to discover, during an RE in-service course, that Muslim children also learn stories about Adam, Noah, Abraham, Mary and Jesus.

All this seems to make an already complex subject even more complicated, but it also emphasizes the need to follow the golden rule and ensure that teachers specify that we are learning about the Bible as believed by Christians. Fortunately, young children seem much better able than adults to cope with diversity, so it is probably the case that the earlier pupils are introduced to these facts the better.

3 A study of the Christian Bible raises very important issues about the relationship between Christianity and Judaism. Like all parent/offspring relationships, that between Christianity and Judaism has been and is very mixed and complex. In a pluralistic world the RE teacher should take the relationship into account.

Jesus, St Paul and the Apostles were Jews and remained Jews throughout their lives, according to biblical evidence. Luke says that the last supper which Jesus ate with his disciples was the Passover meal (Luke 22). Throughout the previous week he had been daily in the Temple (Luke 20 and 21). St Paul's final arrest took place in or near the Jerusalem Temple to which he had gone to fulfil a vow (Acts 21:18–26). The early Church was exclusively Jewish, and when Gentiles were eventually admitted to membership they were required to observe certain rules so that Jewish consciences would not be upset (Acts 15:19–29).

The Bible of the early Church was the Jewish scriptures – not only the Torah, its first five books, but also the sections containing the prophetic books and Psalms, in keeping with the tradition of the Pharisees. It was not until about 180CE that the term 'Old Testament' was first used by Christian authors to refer to them. Jesus and his followers, however, interpreted their Jewish scriptures in a distinctive way. This seems to have begun when Jesus preached his first sermon in his home synagogue at Nazareth. He read:
'The spirit of the Lord is upon me because he has anointed me; he has sent me to announce good news to the poor, to proclaim release for prisoners and recovery of sight for the blind; to let the broken victims go free, to proclaim the year of the Lord's favour', and added: 'Today, in your hearing this text has come true.'
(Luke 4:18–21)

After this the Jewish disciples used their scriptures to persuade their fellow Jews that Jesus was the promised Messiah. So thorough has this use of the 'Old Testament' been that few people of any religion but Judaism are aware that there is any way of reading it other than as a book which is about Jesus. Yet Jews would read the Handel's *Messiah* passages and others quoted in the New Testament, especially in Matthew's Gospel, in a completely different way. Of course, in teaching Christianity, the Old Testament must be taught as part one of the Christian Bible, but this should at least be done in such a way that no one will say, as teachers sometimes still do: 'Oh, yes, we teach Judaism in our school. We spend a lot of time studying the Old Testament'. In any course on Judaism we must be sure to teach the Jewish scriptures, the Tenakh, from their own point of view, with the emphasis and focus being upon the Torah, not the prophets. Some Anglicans still use the Good Friday collect which includes these words: 'Have mercy upon all Jews, Turks, Infidels, and Hereticks, and take from them all ignorance, hardness of heart, and contempt of thy word.'

St Paul tried to make sense of the fact that many of the Jews to whom he preached rejected his message. In his letter to Christians in Rome he suggested that their obstinate hardness of heart, or blindness, was temporary, and an opportunity provided by God for non-Jews to hear the Gospel of salvation. Had the Jews received the Gospel immediately the story of their redemption would have been completed, with the Gentiles left outside. (The account can be found in St Paul's letter to the Romans, chapters 9–11.)

Clearly Paul was unable, emotionally and theologically, to believe that the calling of his people now meant nothing. The author of John's Gospel took a different line. For him, the contribution of the Jews to the purposes of God belonged to the past. Any spirituality they might have had was exhausted. This is the meaning of the wedding at Cana story. Its purpose is theological, as John's narratives always are, and is not merely the story of Jesus attending a marriage celebration. Elsewhere in the Gospel Jesus rounds on Jews who question his authority, telling them: 'Your father is the devil and you choose to carry out your father's desires...You are not God's children, and that is why you will not listen' (John 8:44 and 47, but see the whole chapter). John was writing for a community where dialogue or debate had come to an end and been replaced by vituperation and abuse, as is common in broken relationships.

A common feature of the Gospels is disputes between Pharisees and Jesus. Scribes and Pharisees were teachers and interpreters of the Torah. Men like Jesus who may have been one himself. St Paul certainly was (Philippians 3). These were the men who enabled Judaism to survive the trauma of the Jewish Revolt of 66CE, which resulted in the destruction of the Temple four years later. Most New Testament scholars now accept that the portrait of the Pharisees provided in the Gospels is biased. There were some teachers who shared their strictness, but they should not all be lumped together, any more than football supporters should be described as hooligans or children as ill-mannered. It has been suggested that the hostility towards them found in the Gospels is related more to the tensions between them and Christian leaders in the period when the Gospels were written, after the Revolt. Again, it may have to do with the break-up of relationships. Even if the Pharisees were the legalists described by the evangelists, Christians should not be prevented by it from realizing that Jesus was a Jew, that the arguments are, therefore, domestic, between members of the same family, and that the amazing humanity of the prophets is as much part of Judaism as any legalism. Moreover, the purpose should be not to judge, as the New Testament does, but to understand the tensions. At Key Stage 3 and Key Stage 4 there is plenty of material for studying Christian–Jewish relationships.

In case the seriousness of the situation has still escaped the readers, we close with some words of Martin Luther in his pamphlet *Concerning the Jews and their Lies*:

'Their synagogues or churches should be set on fire and whatever does not burn should be covered or spread over with dirt so that no one may ever be able to see a cinder or stone of it. Their homes should likewise be broken down or destroyed. Their rabbis must be forbidden under threat of death to teach any more. All their cash and valuables of gold and silver ought to be taken from them and put aside for safe-keeping...

To sum up, dear princes and nobles who have Jews in your domains, if this advice of mine does not suit you, then find a better one so that you and we may all be free of this insufferable devilish burden – the Jews.'

4 We need also to respond to the fears of those who feel that if the place of Bible study is reduced to just part of the teaching of Christianity, the pupils will not be introduced to the many biblical stories and images which lay behind so much of western literature and culture in general. While we sympathize with this position, our reply would be that a short time spent studying the Bible well is better than a long time studying it badly.

Research done in the 1960s showed that pupils who had been presented with Bible stories throughout their school career could still leave school not only unable to understand them but also unable even to remember them accurately. This is because they could not see the relevance of them and so quickly switched off. We hope to help pupils understand the place of the Bible in Christianity and thereby encourage them to discover more of its fascinations for themselves. It is not the job of RE to provide 'background information' for English students and there is far more to RE than studying the Bible. We feel, nevertheless, that the approach advocated here will promote more understanding of and respect for biblical literature and a far more open-minded approach to its study.

5 The teacher is faced with a bewildering number of versions of the Bible to use. Choice can be a problem. There are some attractive selections for use at Key Stage 2, such as *Book of Bible Stories*, Tomie de Paola, Hodder and Stoughton, 1990.

We would discourage Key Stage 1 level anthologies which make no pretence of being actual translations and present personal views, usually removing the religious significance altogether. They do not belong to the classroom. Alan Dale's *New World New Testament* (OUP) is usable from Key Stage 2 for more able readers. *Winding Quest* is based on the Old Testament. Both are his selections and translations. We suggest using the Common Bible from Key Stage 3.

6 Finally, we need to tackle the 'Noah's Ark syndrome'.

Many teachers use the story in such varied topics as 'Water', 'Transport', 'Weather' and 'Animals'. In this way they feel that they have introduced children to an understanding of the Bible. We have to ask, however, how much religious education of the kind advocated in this book is really being achieved, and to what extent the story is really about any of these matters. Noah's Ark is, in fact, a story which raises very difficult theological problems: how does one explain the account of God's decision to destroy his creation and start again? (Genesis 6:5–7, 11–13) Teachers usually avoid these issues by avoiding the context and purpose of the story. It could be argued that Noah's Ark has become a popular folk tale which inspires a range of worthwhile activities for children. This, of course, may be admirable – we just have to remember that it is not Religious Education.

Further reading

For the teacher

Many books on the Bible treat it exclusively as the Christians' book. The teacher who wishes to understand the Jewish context of Christianity and something of their view of the Bible can do no better than read *A History of the Jewish Experience*, L Trepp, Behrmann, 1973.*

Exploring a Theme: Special Books, CEM. Plenty of ideas for primary school teachers.
How to Read the New Testament, E Charpentier, SCM Press, 1981.
How to Read the Old Testament, E Charpentier, SCM Press, 1981.
Introduction to Old Testament Study, J H Hayes, SCM Press, 1992.
People of the Book? The Authority of the Bible in Christianity, J Barton, SPCK, 1978.
The Gospels and Jesus, G Stanton, OUP, 1989.

For the classroom

Book of Bible Stories, Tomie de Paola, Hodder and Stoughton, 1990 (Key Stage 2).

Exploring the Bible, P Curtis, Lutterworth Educational, 1984 (Key Stage 3/4).

The Christian Bible, W Owen Cole, Heinemann Educational, 1993 (Key Stage 3/4).

The Christians' Book, P Curtis, Lutterworth Educational, 1984 (Key Stage 3/4).

The Diary of Anne Frank, Pan, 1953. Still in print and still as powerful (Key Stage 3/4).

The Jewish World, D Charing, Macdonald, 1983 (Key Stage 2/3). A very attractive introduction to Judaism for pupils who know nothing about the religion.*

Video

Message from the Memory Banks, with accompanying booklets, *Considering Origins* and *Considering Meanings*, Janet Green, Bible Society, 1989 (Key Stage 4). One hour, in three twenty-minute parts.

This Land of God. One hour. A tour of the land sacred to three religions (Key Stage 3). *

Windows into Experience, Bible Society, Stonehill Green, Westlea, Swindon SN5 7DG. 90 minutes. Interviews with people for whom the Bible is very important. Costly but can be hired. Long, but can be split into a number of bites (Key Stage 4 and upwards). You could try making your own local version.

(* Can be obtained from Jewish Education Bureau; see Appendix 2.)

8 Jesus

Jesus is central to Christianity. Christianity makes unique claims about Jesus and as a result worships him as the supreme revelation of God. Trying to help young children understand Christian beliefs about Jesus is made particularly challenging by the fact that they often encounter references to Jesus in many different contexts, which can be very confusing for them. Teachers may have distant memories of the misunderstandings or picture-images which were created by words or phrases they heard in church or assembly. Many parents and primary school teachers have endearing stories to tell about young children's attempts to make sense of the confusing terms they have encountered. This writer has on video her four-year-old son singing carefully the words to 'Away in a manger', which he had learned for the playgroup nativity play. Being totally fascinated by cars, he sings with gusto about 'the little Ford Jesus'!

We need to be aware of this sort of confusion and to clarify the ideas and concepts in a way which is appropriate for the child's age range.

The aim of Religious Education is to enable pupils to have a fuller understanding of the place of Jesus in Christianity when they leave school than when they arrived. There are two aspects of this understanding: that of claims about the nature of Jesus and that of beliefs about the life of Jesus.

The nature of Jesus

We have already mentioned the importance of an appreciation of the distinctively Christian beliefs about the nature of Jesus for an understanding of the Christian world view. Jesus of Nazareth is revered as a great religious leader in several traditions, but only Christianity worships him as the second person of the Trinity.

In order to explore the centrality of Jesus in Christianity, we can consider some of the titles Christians use to describe him:

Christ

The word 'Christos', which gives Christianity its name, is the Greek form of the Hebrew word 'Messiah', which, in turn, means 'the anointed one'. In the time of Jesus of Nazareth, the belief that God would send his anointed one – that is, his special representative – to bring about God's purpose on earth and usher in a new age, in which God's reign and sovereignty would triumph, had taken a special urgency. There were many different interpretations of the nature and purpose of the Messiah's mission. Many expected a great military leader who would lead Israel to victory against the Roman oppressors and establish a theocracy centred on Jerusalem. We know from the Dead Sea Scrolls that there were other expectations. The Qumran community believed themselves to be the chosen few, who waited in the desert for the Messiah to punish the corrupt priesthood of the Jerusalem Temple. The followers of Jesus believed him to be God's Messiah, and claimed that Jesus showed God's representative to be a servant who established God's purpose through suffering and death, not military force. This claim of the early Christians that Jesus was God's Messiah was very important in their debates with their fellow Jews. As the Church became increasingly Gentile, the title Christ came to have less direct significance. The concepts of Jesus as God's representative, however, establishing God's reign on earth, are still central to Christianity. Most Christians believe that Jesus will return in a Second Coming to bring an end to history as we know it and establish the Kingdom of God on earth. This belief is interpreted in many different ways throughout the Christian tradition.

Lord

The simple phrase 'Jesus is Lord' was probably one of the earliest Christian creeds. The term 'Lord' was used by Jews and Gentiles to denote divine status. Christians believe that Jesus' lordship was revealed in a supreme way through the resurrection. His triumph over evil and death revealed his divine authority. As the Risen Lord, Jesus was not only a person who lived and died, but a real presence with the post-Easter Christian community. The Christian experience of Jesus as Lord led them to claim that Jesus was not only God's Messiah but was to be worshipped as such. Hence the Christian claim that Jesus is both fully human and fully divine – the incarnation of God.

Son of God

The term 'Son of God' was also a phrase which was familiar to both Jews and Gentiles in Jesus' time. Both cultures used it to describe humans who had a very special relationship with and closeness to God. The Christian use of this term, however, was developed to express more specific claims about the relationship between Jesus and God. Christians believe that Jesus is the son of God in a unique way. They believe him to be God's 'only begotten', whose death and resurrection provide salvation from sin. The Christian experience that Jesus was to be worshipped as God, and the Christian claim that God is one, is expressed through the belief in the Trinity – one God known through three aspects or 'persons': Father, Son and Holy Spirit. Jesus as son of God is therefore the second person of the Trinity.

The difficult concept that Jesus is God yet is *with* God is expressed in the first chapter of John's Gospel, verses 1 to 18. Here, however, the writer of John's Gospel uses the Greek term 'Logos', or 'word' to describe Jesus. This was a philosophical term which was very familiar to the original readers.

The life and teachings of Jesus

Many people are surprised by just how little historical record exists of this person who has had so much influence on history itself. There is nothing to suggest that Jesus left any writings. Apart from a few, very general references in ancient history, the only information we have about the life and teaching of Jesus comes from the Gospels. Biblical scholarship has shown that even these contain very little biographical detail. We discuss the special nature of the Gospels in Chapter 7.

We do not believe that this lack of historical evidence should concern us. Such a situation is true of most important figures from the ancient past, and it should seem to remind us that when we are teaching about the life of Jesus we are not dealing with biographical information written from an 'objective' point of view, but presenting the faith claims of a believing community. The 'authority' for these accounts, therefore, lies not in historical research, nor in the teacher as expert, but in the living faith of the Christians who preserved and transmitted them and still recount them today.

When considering the teachings of Jesus we find again that it is not presented in a straightforward and comprehensive way. Christian thinkers have developed a philosophy of ethics out of the records of Jesus' words. There are, however, very few examples of direct ethical teachings in the Gospels. In the first three Gospels, most of Jesus' teaching is either in the form of parables or in the sort of dialogue employed by rabbis of the time – he nearly always answers a question with a question (e.g. Mark 12:14–17, Matthew 9:14–15, Luke 10:25–37).

The parables are a very important part of Jesus' teaching, yet biblical scholarship suggests that they have been much misunderstood by Christian teachers. We discussed this in some detail in Chapter 5. This suggests that teachers should present Jesus' parables not as allegories to be interpreted as moral tales, but as stories which present an analogy to the hearer, providing a challenge and provoking a response. The work of scholars in this field suggests that the challenge that Jesus presented to his hearers was the idea that God was calling them to 'enter the Kingdom of God' – that is, to 'accept God as king' then and there, through Jesus, and that this call was an immediate and urgent one! The audience was also challenged to accept that God was offering this invitation to everyone, even the errant sinners. God's forgiveness was offered to anyone and all who repented could enter the kingdom. This seemed to be a difficult idea to accept for those who believed that they had lived a good life and kept God's laws.

Beliefs in the classroom

Conveying Christianity's beliefs about the nature of Jesus involves dealing with concepts which baffle theologians and philosophers – let alone school children! We would argue, however, that, as with any other difficult concept, children can be prepared for an understanding by laying the foundations and then building on them. Teachers can find educational aids in the ways in which Christians themselves have tried to express their beliefs across the centuries – through symbols, stories and art. The use of pictures in the classroom can sometimes convey ideas even to very young children when it would be almost impossible to put those ideas into words. The stories of Jesus' life are themselves ways of expressing Christian beliefs about Jesus, and they should be taught as such. This, we would argue, is why pupils ought to know them. We do not, however, have the right to assume that the children we teach will want to to accept the Christian perspective for themselves. We do hope, nevertheless, that they will learn to respect them and understand the importance for the culture in which they live.

We will now consider ways in which an understanding of Jesus' place in Christianity can be developed throughout a child's education.

Key Stage 1

Very young children can be introduced to Christian beliefs about Jesus through the use of simple terms such as his 'specialness'. The arrival of Christmas is a good opportunity to show how Christians tell the nativity story to show what Jesus means to them. (Matthew 1 and 2, Luke 1 and 2.) They can also be introduced to relevant stories and teachings which are appropriate for their age range. We would suggest that the accounts of Jesus calling his disciples (Mark 1:16–20 and 11) and Jesus calling Zacchaeus (Luke 19:1–10) are good examples of Jesus' leadership, authority and compassion to use for this age range. Some examples of Jesus' teaching could also be presented in a very simple way. The parables of the Lost Son (Luke 15:11–32) and the Good Samaritan (Luke 10:25–35) are particularly appropriate because of their powerful storyline and immediate message about human relationships.

Key Stage 2

Ideally, children could explore further the place of Jesus in Christianity through a topic such as 'Leaders'. Another possibility is to develop the ideas from work done on the Bible in a topic such as 'Communication' or 'Stories'. An exploration of selected Bible stories could then introduce children to some of the Christian beliefs about Jesus – for instance, the ideas that he was sent by God to help humankind, and that his life, death and resurrection show God at work. The children would meet the Christmas and Easter stories at the relevant times (see Chapters 10 and 11). Most of the remaining narratives about Jesus involve miracle stories. It is important that children understand the purpose of these stories – see Chapter 7. Some examples appropriate for this age range would be:

- Jesus' baptism
- Jesus healing the paralysed man
- Jesus healing on the Sabbath
- Jesus healing Jairus' daughter
- the feeding of the five thousand
- the stilling of the storm.

Children should also be introduced to Jesus' teaching through the parables. The parables found only in Luke seem particularly appropriate to explore with young children – for example, the Lost Son and the Good Samaritan. We would also emphasize the importance of an exploration of Christian art and symbols as a way in which to introduce children to Christian beliefs about Jesus. Resources are suggested at the end of the book.

Key Stage 3

By this stage, pupils should be able to explore Christian beliefs about Jesus within specific RE topics centred on, for instance, 'Christianity' or 'Leaders'. The central Christian claims that Jesus is both fully human and fully divine needs to be emphasized here. Again, ideas can be explored not only through biblical material but also through the use of art and artefacts.

By this time pupils should be aware of the important events in the life of Jesus celebrated by Christians, and could learn about the Sermon on the Mount. They should also, however, be aware that the Gospels are faith statements, rather than biographies, and that they offer different interpretations of some of the stories about Jesus and of his teaching.

Key Stage 4

By the end of Key Stage 4, pupils should be able to understand how the uniquely Christian beliefs about Jesus are expressed through Christian art and worship. They should be aware of the diversity within Christianity, with regard to the interpretation and expression of these beliefs, and should also be able to distinguish between the place of Jesus in Christianity and the respect with which he is regarded in other traditions, for example Islam and Hinduism.

Pupils should now be well acquainted with the series of events given in the Synoptic Gospels' presentation of Jesus' life and teaching. In addition, they can now explore the material in John's Gospel. A study of John's prologue and some of the 'I am' sayings will present pupils with some challenging ideas about the Christian claim about the nature of Jesus.

Further reading

For the teacher

Exploring a Theme: Leaders, CEM. Valuable section on teaching about Jesus for primary school teachers.

For the classroom

Jesus, J F Aylett and R D Holden-Storey, Hodder and Stoughton, 1990 (Key Stage 3/4).

Jesus, T Shannon, Lutterworth, 1982 (Key Stage 3/4).

Jesus and the Birth of the Church, G Windsor and J Hughes, Heinemann Educational, 1990 (Key Stage 3/4).

Jesus World Wide, CEM. Series of six posters of Jesus from different traditions (Key Stage 2 upwards).

Living in the Time of Jesus, P Connolly, OUP, 1983.

The Gospel Story of Jesus, J Thompson, Hodder and Stoughton, 1986 (Key Stage 4/GCSE).

9 Christian worship

This has not usually been covered in Religious Education, as it was thought that daily acts of school worship and the church attendance of children on Sundays would be sufficient. It is now clear that most children have no contact with a church and that school worship is so distinctive in form, by law, that it does not resemble what happens in churches. In fact, Circular 1/94 makes a very clear distinction between school 'collective worship' and the acts of believing communities:

'Worship in schools will necessarily be of a different character from worship amongst a group with beliefs in common.'

(Paragraph 57, page 21)

It is also being recognized by ministers and theologians that there is a need for Christians who are committed and regular church-goers to be educated in the meaning of worship and its component parts, such as prayer, or even perhaps the concept of God, which lies behind and undergirds worship. That is what a school course on worship can provide for all pupils.

For the Christian, worship is the spontaneous response of the believer to God. This might be remembered when we begin to talk about times, places, and the planning and organization of worship – all the things which happen and are important when one human need or activity has to be balanced against another. Individuals may worship spontaneously when and where they like; groups have to make arrangements.

The church as a community

Christians also need to meet somewhere. Jesus and his friends used the Temple and the synagogue, the places of worship of their Jewish religion. When the Temple was destroyed in 70CE, and when Jews who came to believe in Jesus as Messiah and Jews who did not went their separate ways or when communities became totally Gentile, Christians met wherever they could. They worshipped in the open air, in homes, and, in times of danger, in the quarries and caves under Rome and other cities. However, when Solomon built the Temple there was some hesitation in his mind, because he recognized that God did not live in a building made by hands (2 Chronicles 6:18) and Jesus' followers shared that Jewish view. When Christians first used the word 'church' they did not mean a building but the New Israel, the community of women and men called to be followers of Jesus the Messiah. 'Ecclesia' is the Greek word; it lives on in the English word 'ecclesiastical'. Christians were not legally allowed to own property until at least 260CE, when the Emperor Gallienus ended their persecution by his father Valerian I.

The church building

The sites of Christian churches in Britain are often places where Roman or even earlier religious buildings existed, not merely because stones or ruins could be reused, but because the location already had some spiritual significance. It was already sacred to the converts. This sanctity or holiness was often enhanced by the installation of relics and the burial inside the church of saints – men and women whose lives were deeply spiritual. The power that they possessed in their lives was believed to survive their deaths, hence stories like that of St Cuthbert's body surviving in an uncorrupted state in Durham Cathedral, and the medieval cult of saints, which inspired pilgrims to make long and dangerous journeys to Canterbury or Rome.

Churches have attracted patrons who have commissioned artists to decorate them with stained glass windows, altar pieces, tapestries and many other artefacts. Cynics may say that they did it for their own memory to be preserved, but the glory of God came into it as well; church-builders and benefactors should not be looked upon with the eyes of the late 20th century. Those who could be were buried inside the church, the closer to the altar the better. The others were laid to rest in the church yard, facing east, ready for the resurrection of the dead and as near to the altar as possible – just beyond the east end, where the altar stood.

Sunday

In New Testament times (Revelation 1:10) Sunday, the 'Lord's Day', was already special. For Jews the seventh day was a holy day; Christians chose Sunday, on the basis that on the first day God created light and that Jesus was also the light of the world; and also because it was the day when the Apostles received the Holy Spirit at Pentecost (Acts 2). The Roman dedication of the day to the sun, the giver of light, might be another explanation. Yet another was the wish to be different from the Jews.

Forms of worship

There are two main forms of Christian worship, as well as combinations of the two. One focuses on the meal which Jesus shared with his disciples known as the Last Supper (Luke 22). It has many names related to particular denominations: the Mass (Roman Catholic), the Eucharist (Anglican), holy communion (general), the Lord's Supper or communion or breaking of bread (non-conformist or free churches), the divine liturgy (the eastern churches). This form of worship is sacramental; a sacrament is a means of conveying God's grace, his forgiving love and strengthening power.

The second focus is on the Bible, with the act of worship, the service, emphasizing the reading of scripture, a sermon based on it and hymns which are Bible-related. The Bible provides a link between both forms of worship, being used extensively in each.

A third, less dominant form of worship focuses on the Holy Spirit. At one end of this spectrum is the Quaker 'waiting upon the Spirit' in silence; at the other ecstatic pentecostal, charismatic praise resembling, its participants would claim, the worship of the first Christians when they received the Holy Spirit at Pentecost (Acts 2).

Where the Lord's Supper is central to worship, the altar is a central feature of the church. There Jesus' sacrifice is repeated or re-enacted by a priest, a person specially set apart for this purpose. The sacrament can only be celebrated by those ordained to do it, members of these churches would argue. In other churches the pulpit may first catch the eye, indicating that preaching from the Bible is considered to be of most importance. Among such Christians the word 'minister' is more likely to be used than 'priest' to describe the person who leads worship and ministers to the congregation by giving pastoral advice and performing weddings, baptisms and funerals.

Some other aspects of the building may be worth noting. Where the altar is central, there may be a lectern from which the Bible is read, set to the right hand side as the congregation views it; on the other will be the pulpit, from which a sermon is preached. In old churches there were usually no organs so architecturally they don't fit in to the otherwise orderly pattern of the building. Plan I is of this kind of church.

There are variations on the cross shape. Liverpool Roman Catholic cathedral, for example, is the best known altar-focused building in Britain which is round in shape. It symbolizes the congregation gathering around the altar.

Where the pulpit is central (plan II), there is no need for a lectern, as the Bible is read from the pulpit. But between the pulpit and the pews, where the congregation sit, there will be a table. Here the minister conducts the communion service, which may take place monthly or even less frequently, assisted by members of the congregation. In the north of England and Wales such places may be called 'chapels' instead of churches.

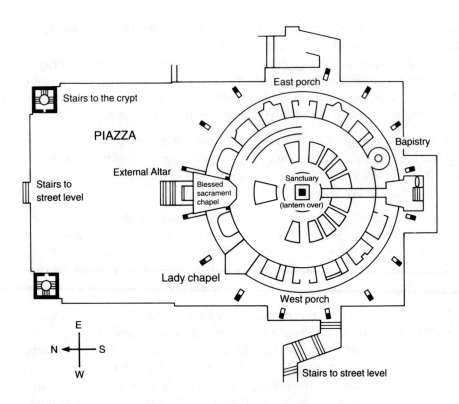

Plan I Plan of Liverpool Metropolitan Cathedral (RC)

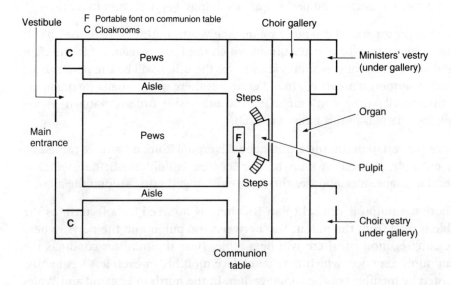

Plan II Plan of a non-conformist, or free, church

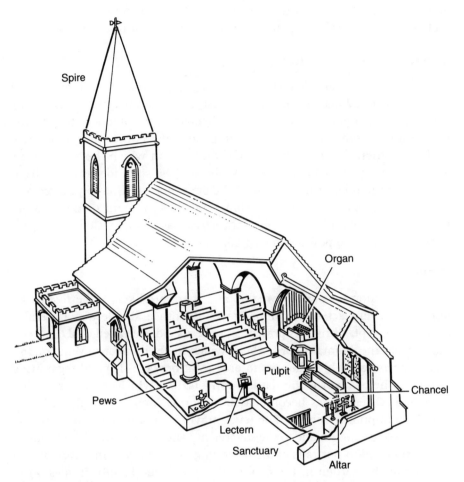

Plan III A cutaway illustration showing the layout of an Anglican or Roman Catholic church

Clergy and ministers

Most denominations now have full-time professional leaders but for a long time the ministers of non-conformist/free churches were men elected from the congregation. (Women ministers belong to the 20th century. Quakers have never had ministers and women have taken leadership roles from the beginning.) 'Clergy' tends to be a term used more by Roman Catholics, Anglicans and eastern Christians, who will sometimes address them as 'Father', indicating that they are the father in God or caring parent of the church community. 'Reverend' is an honorary title given to all ordained men and women, but it should not be used when speaking to them. We might say:

'The Reverend Eli Thomas has come to speak to us today'. But we would then go on to say: 'Mr Thomas is vicar of...', or 'Father Thomas...' if that is his preference. Religious literacy means using the correct forms of address.

The purpose of worship

Worship is more about the relationship with God through Jesus than ways of speaking to clergy-persons. It usually consists of a number of aspects. It may begin with a hymn of praise, a religious song intended to lift the congregation from its concern with mundane affairs into the presence of God. Then there is often a prayer of confession, in which the worshippers acknowledge their inadequacies and failures. The situation has now been created for the relationship between the believers and God to proceed and develop unimpeded, reaching its climax in the sacrament or the sermon, through either of which, as well as the service as a whole, God's grace, his loving presence and power is mediated.

Prayer

This is an important part of worship and there are likely to be five or six prayers in every act of worship. Prayer is both a simple activity and a complex concept. Christians pray because Jesus did. He called God 'Dad', for that is what the Aramaic word 'Abba', which he used, means (Mark 14:36), and he encouraged his followers to pray (Matthew 6:5–15) and regard God as their father. Prayer is the natural conversation which the Christian has with God. Often it has become stylized, formal and seemingly artificial, especially in public worship. For Jews, prayer is an animated conversation with few concessions made to the sovereignty and superiority of God. One of the most beautiful portraits at the beginning of the Bible is the story of God walking in the garden in the cool of the day (Genesis 3:8). It goes on to describe the spoilt relationship between Adam, Eve and God. Hence the need for confession when the worshipper approaches God.

A Christian emphasis has always been upon God as transcendent, and consequently upon prayer. If people stress the immanence of God, meditation may replace prayer, as the practitioner seeks to realize union with the divinity which is within. Some Christians meditate; Quakers have always spoken of the 'inner light' and St Paul wrote about the Holy Spirit living within the Christian.

When we are teaching about prayer or using prayers in school worship we should have this richness in mind, instead of conveying the idea that prayer is a quick fix in the form of a request for ourselves or others. Christian petitionary prayer is sharing God's concern, not bringing to his notice something that he seems to have overlooked!

Hymns and music in worship

As we encounter expressions of religion in which singing does not play a part and may actually meet with disapproval, it might be asked why Christians use music in worship. The answer lies in Judaism, and especially in the Book of Psalms, the hymn book of the Temple. After the Last Supper Jesus sang one of the psalms associated with Passover (Mark 14:26), and he would have sung others whenever he approached Jerusalem as a pilgrim. Many Christian hymns are versions of the psalms; others are inspired by events in the life of Jesus or his teachings.

Dance is sometimes also an ingredient in worship. Again, the justification is Jewish practice. King David danced in front of the Ark which contained the tablets of the Torah (2 Samuel 6:16), though his daughter, Michal, despised him for it. Our puritan past and the association of dance with pre-Christian forms of religion may explain why many Britons tend not to favour the use of dance in worship.

Sermons

Sermons are another part of the Jewish tradition. Teachers like Jesus (Luke 4) explained the meaning of the Torah to their disciples and synagogue congregations. Scriptures are not dead letters – they, too, are means of grace.

Teaching suggestions

There is no dearth of information to be gathered and concepts to be explored in worship throughout the Key Stages. Spiralling is the great challenge: going deeper each time we return to the subject and always remembering that the church is a place of worship, the home of a community of believers.

Key Stage 1

A local church is an obvious starting place. A visit is essential. For many children it will be a new and perhaps threatening experience. If there are some church members among the parents and a friendly minister who has already met the class they may be reassured by having them as their companions on the visit. It is important for us to have an awareness of what knowledge, concepts and attitudes children bring to their exploration of religion; this is just as important for our work in RE as knowledge of children's numeracy. A discussion about the big place with a clock/spire/tower in Church Street, listening to what they have to say with as little comment as possible (though prompting may be necessary), might be very edifying. On the visit the children might be allowed to look around in groups for some time with the minimum of guidance before their attention is drawn to a particular feature, such as the big book, the Bible, from which those who come to church hear about Jesus. The minister might simulate a baptism to show that the building is a place where things happen and how membership of the church begins. Children should become aware that this is the place where some people come to worship God.

Suggestions about introducing children to the concept of God and the idea of prayer are made at the end of this chapter.

Key Stage 2

Who built the church, when, why, and why on this spot may link the church with what is being done in History and/or Geography. Religious Education will concentrate on when people go (why Sunday?), what they do when they are there, and the meaning of the terms which will be used. There may be opportunities to invite members of the congregation into school to discuss what the church means to them, for ministers to describe their work and why they decided to become clergy, for older people to reminisce about their wedding or the baptisms of their children. For most children what is being talked about may still be very strange, including mention of God.

Knowledge of what happens in worship should be covered at this stage, perhaps with the aid of simulations. The names of the different parts of a church should be known, as well as the arrangement of at least an Anglican/Roman Catholic and non-conformist or free church, because this knowledge is necessary for the development of further study and understanding of worship. Learning these facts should be as enjoyable as possible. Perhaps doing plans of churches on computer could make the exercise pupil-friendly. Certain rites should be known and understood as far as possible – both infant and believer's baptism, holy communion, weddings and also funerals – and humanized as far as possible by Christians sharing their ideas and experiences.

Key Stage 3

At this stage, the meaning of prayer and the contents of some hymns can be studied to explore their theology, what they say to Christians and what they mean to them, as well as the basic question 'What is worship?' The significance of the sacraments – the seven of the Roman Catholic Church, not just two (baptism and holy communion) – should be understood. Sacraments convey power, God's grace – that is their purpose. It is not easy to transmit this notion. There may be everyday life links; for example, owning the autographed album of a pop group, or just seeing a pop star. We sometimes hear of a person recovering from a coma after being played a tape by their favourite group, or even after one of them visiting them in the intensive care unit. All analogies are inadequate, but they may go some way towards helping children who are not religious to say: 'Ah, I can see what that might do for them!' or 'I know how they must have felt when they couldn't take communion'.

Key Stage 4

All the questions which may have come to mind as you read the first part of this chapter can be dealt with now, especially why Christians worship God, and how they do, and what 'God' means to them theologically and in their everyday lives. The meaning of the Apostles' Creed, which is used in worship in many churches, should be understood by the end of Key Stage 4. Pupils should also know how symbols and metaphorical language are used by religions. Metaphor is very important in Christian thought and worship. God is called 'Father', but that is not to be taken literally. When some Christians speak about being satisfied by the food which they receive at a communion service, they are talking about spiritual satisfaction, which is as necessary to them as full stomachs. The transition from taking things literally to understanding ideas metaphorically is as important in literature as in the development of religious understanding, but it is rarely achieved.

The spiritual life of the Iona community or Taizé or similar groups, including Christian monastic communities and ashrams in India and the devotional life of living monks and nuns, might provide other ways of approaching Christian worship and spirituality. Visits to Buddhist communities in Britain often prove stimulating. Going to a Christian monastery should be equally valuable.

Issues

God and prayer

Have you watched reception or pre-school children at their first assembly when a teacher says 'Let us pray'? Glances along the line, and if no help is to be found there, a quick look behind. Someone puts hands together and closes eyes (it may be a teacher) and children follow suit, closing them tightly as though they were going to get soap in them!

Christian parents worship God all the time, and their children will copy them, but a point comes when they need to formulate their own beliefs about God and prayer. How many parents, clergy and teachers help children grow into a mature faith?

The teacher is an educator and must have a particular concern for pupils who come from homes which are non-religious. Believers often cannot remember when they first heard the word 'God' or when they learned the Lord's Prayer. These and the word 'Jesus' were part of their under-five vocabulary. It may be hard for them to put themselves in the shoes of children with the opposite experience or of something in between, but that is where most of our pupils are.

Key Stage 1

Guidelines in Agreed Syllabuses often state that children should have 'some understanding of God and the meaning and purpose of prayer'. How can we help them to obtain it? Where can we begin?

First, we would suggest that we listen. If God has been mentioned in assembly children may be talking about him/her/it (they may already have settled for the pronoun 'he'), trying to make some sense of what has been heard. This might take the form of discussion as children sit on the carpet.

Secondly, we might raise the question if no one is discussing it. 'This morning Mrs Harvey said God loves everybody. Who *is* God?'

When we know where children are, we can begin helping them on their journey of conceptual development.

The awareness of God often comes to believers as they ponder the deep questions of life, its joys and its pain, its beauty and its ugliness. The 'wow' or even 'ugh' situations that we find ourselves in with our class might provide opportunities for taking them along the path of realizing that the existence of God is a real issue for many people rather than something theoretical. (Some of the books in Further reading, Chapter 5, may help.)

Perhaps we can now begin formal exploration of Christian belief at Key Stage 1 by using such material as Psalm 23, the Lost Coin and the Lost Sheep (Luke 15). The concepts in these biblical passages are not easy, but they may be preferable to telling the class that God cares for them like a father. Many people have only wonderful memories of their fathers, but there are many infants who have never even seen theirs. What are the implications of this when it comes to teaching children 'Our Father'? We should also think about how we can help them understand the Christian concept of God as parent when their own family experiences may not be happy ones.

Children and prayer is a difficult matter to write about. The needs which adults find met by prayer are often answered for children by the grown-ups in their life. When five-year-olds are injured or have done something wrong it would be cruel to point them to God and tell them to pray about it. They need a cuddle. We would rather encourage children to reflect upon what we have been talking about, maybe with the help of a poem, than to say, 'Now let us thank God for...'.

Teaching children about prayer might begin with the notion that God is someone we can talk with and that when Christians go to church they talk with God. Thinking about and discussing some prayers and hymns that Christians use which go beyond asking or even thanking, and towards a partnership with God, might be helpful.

Finally, though this piece is written with infant children primarily in mind, we must always remember that continuity and progression are as important in Religious Education as in any other subject. Understanding what God, prayer and worship mean to Christians should be essential aspects of Key Stages 2, 3 and 4 work. The result should be 16-year-olds who have a mature understanding of what Christians believe.

Appendix

One way of triggering off discussion about the concept of God might be to use a story such as the call of the disciples and to end it by saying that Jesus wanted his friends to go with him to tell people how God wanted them to live. Who is God? Why was Jesus able to tell people about God? Not because he was the 'son of God', but because he spent so much time with God (prayer) that he felt he knew God's mind and will (adult language and concepts, of course). Stories such as those mentioned above illustrate what he taught about God: mainly forgiveness and love.

Further reading

For the teacher

Contact with local churches is important. They will be able to inform you of hymn books, prayer books and liturgies which they may use, particularly on special occasions, e.g. Good Friday, Easter Day.

Anyone There?, Brenda Lealman, CEM, 1985. Can be used at Key Stage 3 but is likely to be useful to teachers generally.
Investigating Belief in God, K R Chappell, Edward Arnold, 1985 (Key Stage 3/4). Of interest to teachers. Somewhat confessional but emphasizes religious experience.
RE Today, summer 1988, vol 5 no 3. Gives special attention to teaching about God.

For the classroom

Christian Communities, A Brown, Lutterworth Educational, 1982 (Key Stage 3/4).

Christian Experience, C Erricker, Lutterworth Educational, 1982 (Key Stage 3/4).

Christian Worship, J Rankin, Lutterworth Educational, 1982 (Key Stage 3/4).

Colin's Baptism, O Bennett, Hamish Hamilton, 1986 (Key Stage 2).

I am an Anglican, M Killigray, Franklin Watts, 1986 (Key Stage 2).

I am a Greek Orthodox, M Roussou, Franklin Watts, 1985 (Key Stage 2).

I am a Pentacostalist, B Pettenuzzo and C Fairclough, Franklin Watts, 1986 (Key Stage 2).

I am a Roman Catholic, B Pettenuzzo, Franklin Watts, 1986 (Key Stage 2).

Something of a Saint, D M Owen, SPCK, 1990. Lives and prayers of 52 famous Christians in all ages (Key Stage 2/3).

The Pope and the Vatican, R Thomas and J Stutchbury, Macmillan Australia, 1986 (Key Stage 2).

Video

Buildings and Beliefs. English Heritage Education Service, Keysign House, 429 Oxford Street, London W1R 2HD. 20 minutes. Historical. The story of the development of All Saints, York, but can be used in RE if one looks at the purpose and religious function of the building (from Key Stage 3).

Lourdes: Pilgrimage and Healing, St Paul Multimedia Productions, Middle Green, Langley, Slough SL3 6BS. 40 minutes. Can be divided into several sections (Key Stage 4 and upwards).

10 Christian festivals: Easter and other festivals

The focus of Christian festivals is Jesus. Because of the part which Christmas plays in the life of most schools, echoing its importance as a major celebration in British society, it will be given a chapter to itself. In this section we shall consider the significance of festivals in the life of religions and then look at the greatest Christian festival: Easter.

Festivals generally have at least four elements:

1 the story or stories
2 the meaning(s)
3 the religious aspects which are special to the believer
4 the secular celebration, including developments and customs. This is usually something which most people can enjoy whether they are of the faith or outside it. We may know Jewish friends who send Christians Christmas cards, Sikhs who put up Christmas trees, and we may give Divali presents, attend a Divali bonfire, and share the meal of fast-breaking with Muslim friends one Ramadan evening, but Christians will not usually go to the mosque for prayers. This belongs to category three: things which are special for believers. (In using 'secular' we admit it may not be completely appropriate. For the believer there may be no distinction between aspects three and four.)

In British schools the distinction between three and four, if there is one at all, is blurred. School worship is based on the assumption that everyone is a Christian unless they opt out, and if they do they run the risk of seeming odd or awkward. But there is a distinction. When we *teach* about festivals in Religious Education, instead of celebrating them as a school community (which we may well do), we must draw the line between three and four very clearly, otherwise the specialness of the festival for the believer will be lost, and with it the recognition that a vital element, that of commitment, is involved. Religious Education is about helping believers and those outside a faith to *understand* its festivals.

Easter

The story

The story element of Easter begins with the entry of Jesus into Jerusalem on what is known as Palm Sunday (Mark 11:1–12). In it his popularity and the joyful support of his followers is presented in a way which provides an intentional contrast with the cry of 'Crucify him' (Mark 15:13) and the disciples' desertion (Mark 14:15). Hence the palm crosses which Christians receive on Palm Sunday. (NB Ukranian Roman Catholics use willow branches.) The other main incidents are the overturning of the tables of the money-changers in the Temple (Mark 11:15–19), the Last Supper, which includes Judas's betrayal (Mark 11:10–50), the washing of the disciples' feet by Jesus (John 13:1–11), the prayer in the Garden of Gethsemane (Mark 14:32–42), and the arrest and trial of Jesus (Mark 14:53–15:20). Then comes the crucifixion itself (Mark 14:21–42), and, finally, the resurrection (Mark 16:1–8 and the final chapters of the other Gospels).

There is plenty of story material here. Notice that not all episodes are covered in every Gospel. The authors have their own reasons for what they select and how they tell the story. Mark may be the earliest and most straightforward account to use.

Meaning

Like the best stories Easter has many meanings. At one level it is about human unreliability and human courage, but its distinctiveness for Christians lies in such things as the victory of love and goodness over the forces of evil; the vindication of all the things Jesus claimed about himself – to be God's representative, the Messiah, God's son, to be the one who died for the sins of humanity past, present and future, and who gives eternal life to those who believe in him. For the Christian, belief that death is not the end of life and that suffering can be overcome is based upon the triumph of Jesus and his resurrection. The story of Easter was not one of resuscitation: the Gospel writers go out of their way to make the point that Jesus really was dead. The end of the Easter story, the Ascension, implicitly affirms this. Jesus does not go to Egypt or Kashmir to live out his days; he goes to his Father.

Christianity stands or falls on the belief that Jesus really died and was raised to life.

Religious aspects and celebrations

The celebration of Easter which is special to believers is mainly attendance at worship, Holy Week services culminating in those of Easter Day. Some will also take part in vigils and Good Friday processions. The general celebrations of Easter are well enough known. In Britain they take the form of giving Easter eggs and perhaps sending cards with spring scenes on them.

Easter seems to be the most difficult Christian festival to teach. Reasons teachers give for this include:

1 talking to children about someone dying
2 telling them about the resurrection, about which the teacher is perhaps uncertain, or which the teacher does not believe. 'How can I answer the questions that the children may ask?' is how it is often put.

The basic solution has been given previously. We need to distance ourselves from the questions by remembering that we are talking and teaching about what Christians believe. The answer to the question 'Did Jesus really rise from the dead?' should be, 'That is what Christians believe. If you go to a church on Easter Day you will find them celebrating it'. Though it may be difficult to convince ourselves, the children we teach and their parents, the question of the resurrection, and teaching about it, is really no different in kind to the deliverance from Egypt which Jews celebrate at Passover, or the Night Journey and Ascension of the Prophet Muhammad (pbuh) to Heaven which Muslims observe on 26 Rajab, or the birth of the son of God which Christians celebrate at Christmas. (Why do we find no difficulty in telling the Christmas story?) Each is a story of a divine activity which may be incredible to the outsider but must be taught from the perspective of the insider, the believer.

Teaching suggestions

Key Stage 1

Teachers are often encouraged to approach Easter implicitly, through the exploration of the season of spring and the new life which is associated with it. This could lead to the accusation of sowing the seeds of faith by an appeal to nature. We do well to celebrate spring with young children, but we do so because of its own intrinsic worth. In religious terms spring and the hare, not the bunny, have to do with the worship of Eostre, the Anglo-Saxon goddess, not Jesus.

We would want to argue that details of the Good Friday/Easter material lie so far beyond the experience of children at this stage that it is best avoided. The Easter garden, which is found in many churches and often made by the younger children, might provide a focus for three pieces of information: people who didn't like Jesus killed him (the cross), his friends buried him (the tomb), but Christians believe that he came back to life three days later (the empty tomb and the other features which are sometimes added). Some of the things that Christian children in some cultures do at this time might be done in class, e.g. painting eggs. Within the religion Key Stage 1 is the time when children learn by doing.

Key Stage 2

This is the period of instruction in faith communities. By now children should know something of the life and ministry of Jesus (see chapter 8). Its climax should follow. The story from Palm Sunday to the arrest can be told as a series of episodes. There is plenty of excitement – the dramatic entry into Jerusalem, the nightly slipping away to the safety of Bethany, the care Jesus apparently took to keep the location of the Last Supper a secret (Mark 14:12–16) suggests that even the disciples didn't know the place; they were told to follow a man who would be carrying a water pot), the foot-washing and the meal. The shock of the arrest took the disciples by surprise so that they fled in disarray and despair. All this can be told as in the Bible, probably using Mark's account, at least in the main, or, if it is familiar, from the point of view of the boy Mark, who probably is mentioned in Mark 14:51, or Simon Peter.

The sequence might be:

1 Palm Sunday
2 cleansing the Temple (perhaps left till Key Stage 3, only because it can take attention away from the main theme of the story, but not if the irony of situation can be brought out)
3 preparing for Passover
4 washing the disciples' feet
5 the shared meal
6 the arrest and Peter's failure
7 the crucifixion
8 the various resurrection accounts. Not all, perhaps, but certainly the one which reinstated Peter (John 21), should be included as a follow-up to the story of the denial. (Mark's Gospel is apparently incomplete, as a glance at the last chapter in most Bibles will show. John 21 is obviously an afterthought to that Gospel, which seems to stop at the end of chapter 20. John 21 fits one of the endings of Mark.)

The biblical material can be linked with what Christians do: the receiving of Palm crosses in church on the Sunday before Easter, the British monarch's and Pope's practices on Maundy Thursday (these could be recorded on video during the previous year, as the school holidays have probably begun by the middle of Holy Week, if not earlier), Good Friday processions, (in Spain and some other countries there are processions every day) and the various ways in which Easter Day is celebrated by Christians. The use of video would appear almost essential as part of the learning process.

Finally, one can look at the meaning of secular customs which have spilled over into the community at large – especially Easter eggs, hot-cross buns and simnel cake – and what they signify. Some, like the hare becoming a rabbit, are examples of pre-Christian practices being taken over by the new religion.

The celebration of Easter in other countries might provide a thought-provoking alternative to the experiences of British children, especially if it can be based on videos, articles from the National Geographical journal and personal observations. (See the video list from Articles of Faith and the *Believe it or Not* ITV series.) There is scope at the upper end of this Key Stage for thinking about the feelings of Peter, the women and even Judas.

Key Stage 3

This is the time for reflection upon the meaning of the events celebrated in the festival in more detail, with the children looking at the Bible material themselves. Hymns, poetry and paintings inspired by the events of Easter could be studied to analyze their meaning and how it is achieved.

The question of how Christians interpret the resurrection could be introduced. For most, but not all, the bodily resurrection of Jesus is regarded as literal fact, like the virginal conception which begins the Jesus story. Others, however, believe it to be a spiritual experience enjoyed by his followers (NB Jesus did not present himself to Pilate or the High Priests to prove his point!), the kind of experience which Christians since then and today claim to have of the one they call their 'Risen Lord'. For all Christians the resurrection is a reality and however they understand the resurrection accounts, they are united in agreeing that 'Jesus lives' and this should be made clear.

Key Stage 4

At this stage it ought to be possible to concentrate solely on what the crucifixion and resurrection mean, looking at such passages as I Corinthians 15 and taking it for granted that the stories are known.

Good Friday was once a time when some Christians showed their zeal by making life unpleasant or even dangerous for Jews. Perhaps because Christianity was winning many converts among the Gentiles by the time the Gospels were written, it is usually the Jews who are blamed for Jesus' death. Pilate, the man with the authority to stay or order the execution, bows to their pressure. Care should be taken in teaching about Holy Week so as not to endorse or transmit the prejudices of the past.

Pentecost

Pentecost is the next most significant festival for Christians. The Jewish festival of Pentecost or Weeks (Shavuot), coming six weeks after Passover, commemorated the giving of the Torah at Sinai. At the Pentecost following the resurrection the Apostles preached that God had given his spirit to those who put their faith in Jesus the Christ. It became the birthday of the Church, the New Israel. When it is taught, this is what should be emphasized, not the strange story of the Apostles speaking in different languages and their hearers, Jews from throughout the Roman world, being able to understand them.

Teaching suggestions

Key Stage 1

Simply mention it as the day when the Apostles began their preaching, so it is regarded as the Church's birthday.

Key Stage 2

The story: Peter the coward becoming Peter the preacher, standing up in the Temple and telling the crowd who had gathered there for Shavuot that Jesus had risen and was the Messiah. The celebration: more in the past than now, perhaps, it was the time when new converts, dressed in white (hence Whitsuntide), were baptized. Confirmations in some denominations may be held just before Pentecost so that the new members of the church can take their first communion at Pentecost. It should be possible to examine the meaning of Pentecost through these practices.

Key Stage 3

The focus should be entirely upon the symbolic meaning of Pentecost.

Key Stage 4

After reminding pupils of the story, study should concentrate on the concept of the Holy Spirit.

Other festivals

Ascension, Corpus Christi, Ash Wednesday and Lent, Epiphany, Advent and other occasions in the Christian year can be taught if and when it seems desirable. Often circumstances will be important in determining what and when: for example, at Corpus Christi, Arundel Roman Catholic Cathedral is decorated with a carpet of flowers. This might prompt a teacher at least to refer to it at Key Stage 3 or to discuss its significance in relationship to the eucharist at Key Stage 4 if working in West Sussex. Elsewhere, except in Roman Catholic schools, the festival might be ignored.

The Ascension (Acts 1:1–11) is popular in denominational schools. A school service would once have been followed by a holiday for the rest of the day. However, we must ask what Key Stage 1 and Key Stage 2 are likely to make of it. Perhaps 'Beam me up Scotty!' is the nearest thing in their experience! Certainly, Jesus must have been frustrated by this final failure of his friends to understand his mission. We would leave the story to Key Stage 3, when its purpose can be examined. It is a tidy way of bringing the resurrection appearance accounts to a close and of explaining that the son of God, his work done, has returned to the Father.

There are many festivals associated with Mary, the mother of Jesus, which are observed by Roman Catholics especially. These will be covered when they occur in Roman Catholic schools. In others they may be ignored. They could contribute to a topic in its own right at Key Stage 3, probably on the place of the Virgin Mary in Christianity.

At some point – the transition from Key Stage 3 to Key Stage 4, perhaps – it might be convenient to tabulate the main items in the Christian year, from Advent to Advent. (The Christian calendar is covered in *Festivals in World Religions*, ed. Alan Brown, Longman; *The Christian World*, Alan Brown, MacDonald and *Christianity*, W Owen Cole, Stanley Thornes.)

Further reading

For the teacher

Christianity, W Owen Cole, Stanley Thornes, 1989.

Festivals, Family and Food, D Carey and J Large, Hawthorn Press, 1982. Ideas for Key Stage 1/2.

Festivals in World Religions, ed. Alan Brown, Longman, 1994. An academic introduction. (NB The author of the section on Muslim festivals is very dissatisfied with the editing of his essay, which cannot be considered reliable.)

Home, School and Faith, David Rose, David Fulton Publishers, 1992. Extends beyond an examination of festivals but includes them.

The Christian Year, J C J Metford, Thames and Hudson, 1991. A study of the nature and origins of the Christian calendar.

The Christian World, Alan Brown, MacDonald, 1984.

The Way of the Cross from Latin America, Adolfo Esquival, CAFOD. Fourteen pictures of Roman Catholic meditation on Jesus' last journey. Links with ecological concerns, so useful also in Chapters 13 and 15 (Key Stage 3/4).

For the classroom

Easter in Greece, J Vaughan, Macmillan, 1988 (Key Stage 1/2).

Easter in the Orthodox and Western Traditions, a teacher's pack. South London Multifaith RE Centre, Kilmore Road, London SE23. From the same source: *The Orthodox Church*, a teacher's pack.

Religion through Festivals, R O Hughes, Longman, 1989 (Key Stage 2/3).

Video

The Way to Light, St Paul Multimedia Productions. 20 minutes. A meditation on the passion and resurrection of Jesus, based on the art of Marcello Silvestri. Could help older pupils reflect on the meaning of Easter for Christians (Key Stage 4 and upwards).

11 Christian festivals: Christmas

The most celebrated and least understood festival

This is a conclusion based on work with students and conversations with teachers. Even students going to college to take Religious Studies as their main subject have been known to be ignorant of the meaning of the festival, beyond the fact that it celebrates the birth of Jesus. They may be unaware of which Gospels tell the story. The details are likely to be confused and the number of wise men categorically given as three. Some of these matters probably shouldn't concern us too much, though teachers ought to possess accurate information.

The main reason for ignorance is that Christmas is celebrated rather than taught. Of course, the festival should be celebrated and enjoyed by as many children as feel that they can join in, but it should also form part of the Religious Studies syllabus.

The story

Christmas begins with the two nativity stories, which are printed below. When you have read the accounts you might like to break them down into subheadings.

Luke

2 In those days a decree went out from Caesar Augustus that all the world should be enrolled. ²This was the first enrolment, when Quirin'i-us was governor of Syria. ³And all went to be enrolled, each to his own city. ⁴And Joseph also went up from Galilee, from the city of Nazareth, to Judea, to the city of David, which is called Bethlehem, because he was of the house and lineage of David, ⁵to be enrolled with Mary, his betrothed, who was with child. ⁶And while they were there, the time came for

Matthew

2 Now when Jesus was born in Bethlehem of Judea in the days of Herod the king, behold, wise men from the East came to Jerusalem, saying, ²'Where is he who has been born king of the Jews? For we have seen his star in the East, and have come to worship him.' ³When Herod the king heard this, he was troubled, and all Jerusalem with him; ⁴and assembling all the chief priests and scribes of the people, he inquired of them where the Christ was to be born.

her to be delivered. [7]And she gave birth to her first-born son and wrapped him in swaddling cloths, and laid him in a manger, because there was no place for them in the inn. [8]And in that region there were shepherds out in the field, keeping watch over their flock by night. [9]And an angel of the Lord appeared to them, and the glory of the Lord shone around them, and they were filled with fear. [10]And the angel said to them, 'Be not afraid; for behold, I bring you good news of a great joy which will come to all the people; [11]for to you is born this day in the city of David a Saviour, who is Christ the Lord. [12]And this will be a sign for you: you will find a babe wrapped in swaddling cloths and lying in a manger.' [13]And suddenly there was with the angel a multitude of the heavenly host praising God and saying, [14]'Glory to God in the highest, and on earth peace among men with whom he is pleased!' [15]When the angels went away from them into heaven, the shepherds said to one another, 'Let us go over to Bethlehem and see this thing that has happened, which the Lord has made known to us.' [16]And they went with haste, and found Mary and Joseph, and the babe lying in a manger. [17]And when they saw it they made known the saying which had been told them concerning this child; [18]and all who heard it wondered at what the shepherds told them. [19]But Mary kept all these things, pondering them in her heart. [20]And the shepherds returned, glorifying and praising God for all they had heard and seen, as it had been told them.

[5]They told him, 'In Bethlehem of Judea; for so it is written by the prophet: [6]"And you, O Bethlehem, in the land of Judah, are by no means least among the rulers of Judah; for from you shall come a ruler who will govern my people Israel."' [7]Then Herod summoned the wise men secretly and ascertained from them what time the star appeared; [8]and he sent them to Bethlehem, saying, 'Go and search diligently for the child, and when you have found him bring me word, that I too may come and worship him.' [9]When they had heard the king they went their way; and lo, the star which they had seen in the East went before them, till it came to rest over the place where the child was. [10]When they saw the star, they rejoiced, exceedingly with great joy; [11]and going into the house they saw the child with Mary his mother, and they fell down and worshipped him. Then, opening their treasures, they offered him gifts, gold and frankincense and myrrh. [12]And being warned in a dream not to return to Herod, they departed to their own country by another way.

Meaning

Christmas means many things to Christians. Jesus' birth represents hope, love, forgiveness and light, in the sense of Jesus being the Light of the World. At Key Stage 1 a foundation can be laid by conveying the idea that Jesus was a very special baby, which is why many people celebrate his birthday every year and why shepherds and the wise men visited him. At Key Stage 2 his special importance will have been noted through other stories which children will have learned about him, but they might also note, in a topic on 'Calendars' or 'Time', how Christian influence has resulted in time being divided into BC/AD. The songs of Mary and Simeon address themselves to the significance of the child. It is, however, at Key Stage 4 that the variety of meanings given to the incarnation can be explored fully. They are summed up in the opening chapter of John's Gospel and in such words as 'God as in Christ reconciling the world to himself' (2 Corinthians 5:19). Here we encounter the term 'Christ'. Much of the significance of Jesus for the first Christians is summed up in this word, which is explained briefly on pages 81–2. It is derived from 'Christos', the Greek word for the Hebrew 'Messiah', 'the anointed one'. At the time of Jesus many Jews expected God to send his anointed one to deliver them from the oppression of the Romans. The hope is expressed in Mary's song but she and Simeon also express the Christian belief that the messiahship of Jesus is one of a servant. It is lowliness which is to be exalted in him, not regal might. This is implicit in the story of Herod (Matthew 2).

Handling the birth of Jesus the Messiah is one of the many occasions when the teacher needs to be careful that in presenting the Christian story the Jewish one is not being distorted. A section is devoted to this issue and warning signs are posted at various points in this book (see pages 77 and 78). Abler and older Key Stage 4 and above pupils could profitably examine the birth and infancy narratives as portrayals of the Christian concept of messiahship and as prologues to the two Gospels which contain them. When they have studied the Passion narratives of the same Gospels they might return to these early chapters again to look at how the cross is foreshadowed in them (e.g. the gifts of the Magi). The idea of reconciliation, which has been mentioned above, is present in the concept of the virgin birth, which it is also necessary to study at Key Stage 4. The universal nature of Jesus' significance is implicit in the fact that the wise men were non-Jews, and in the annunciation to the shepherds.

Religious aspects special to the believer

The stories of festivals and their meanings are obviously important to the believer but there are also things which they do. Christians may prepare for

Christmas with special services during Advent, which begins on the Sunday nearest St Andrew's Day (30 November), the first Sunday of the ecclesiastical year. It is a time of penitence, though fasting is not common among western Christians. In eastern churches the fast may have begun as a preparation for baptisms, which took place at Epiphany, 6 January. The lighting of Advent candles and the anticipation of Christmas Day have pushed penitence into the background in the minds of many Christians, though sermons relate to serious matters, such as the Second Coming of Jesus and the Final Judgement. Christmas Day, of course, is an occasion for special services and the singing of seasonal hymns. All these dimensions of Christmas should be studied at appropriate times. Younger children might visit a church decorated with a tree and see the crib.

Developments and general celebration

No one knows the actual date of Jesus' birth – even the year was only calculated centuries later, by someone who got it wrong! Arguments persist as to when it happened (between about 6BCE and 4CE). As for 25 December, that was about the time when the birth of Mithras and celebrations to Saturn were held. When Christianity ousted them in popular favour it adopted and Christianized the existing celebrations. (Something to discuss at Key Stage 4.) It was Easter, not Christmas, that Christians considered important in the first three centuries.

Festivals often include a general element of celebration in the way that they are observed. For obvious reasons Jews will not celebrate the birthday of 'Christ' and Jehovah's Witnesses will not, but for most Britons, including Hindus and Sikhs and many Muslims, who honour Jesus as a prophet, it is likely to be a cultural festival, as Diwali is for most people in India, regardless of their religion. How Christians keep Christmas spills over into the cultural celebration, so that teachers may find it difficult to distinguish between that which belongs to a household of faith and that which is enjoyed by the general population, but they should be aware of the distinction, as they would be if teaching about the festivals of another religion.

Now we are in a position to decide what of the stories should be told to children at Key Stages 1, 2 and 3. Please write down your choices before reading ours.

We would proceed as follows:

Key Stage 1: Mary is expecting a baby.
She and her husband have to make a journey.
All the accommodation is occupied. The birth presumably takes place in a stable, as the baby is laid in a manger.
Visitors come, shepherds and some men from the east who brought presents.

Key Stage 2: in addition to the above:
The baby was given a special name, Jesus.
The Herod story, but not necessarily the slaughter of the innocents.

Key Stage 3: Mary's song might be learned – it should certainly be known, and perhaps some musical renderings of it heard. So also the story of Simeon and his song.

At the top end of the stage the concept of angels (in the Greek simply 'messengers') should be understood.

The stories should be known in full, apart form the virginal conception, which would be kept back not because of any prudery but because it is an important concept which should be understood at the stage (4) when pupils can begin to investigate the theological purpose, rather than concentrate on the fact.

The link with John the Baptist might be included now, so long as it does not detract from the primary aims of knowing and understanding the stories of the birth of Jesus.

Teaching suggestions

Key Stage 1

Here topics might be:

- birthdays (though note that Jehovah's Witnesses and some Asian cultures don't observe them)
- babies
- homes and families
- journeys
- light.

Through reflecting upon their own experiences and those of other children – the preparations for the birth of a baby, the excitement, visits by relatives – the scene can be set for the birth of Jesus. The need to go on a journey when all the preparations for a normal birth at home have been completed adds a certain piquancy.

Hopefully, children will have come to feel that the birth of Jesus was real and that, for Christians, Jesus is special, which is why they still celebrate it.

Key Stage 2

Any of the topics used at Key Stage 1 could be used, of course, but with attainment targets which ensure progression. These would relate to the practices and traditions associated with Christmas, and what they express.

Examples of topics which would enable these to be explored are:

- calendars – exploring generally the different kinds of calendars: lunar, solar, school years, fiscal years, our own calendar (probably beginning with our birthday), religious calendars; leading to why, when Christmas came to be celebrated, it was decided to observe it on 25 December (Gregorian calendar) and 6 January (Julian, which eastern churches still use). Why Christians began to keep Christmas is something that could arise out of this
- customs – the tree, lights, foods. None of these is Christian in origin, but most have been given Christian meanings. How did these and other customs become associated with Christmas? What symbolism attaches to them now? Why did the Puritans attempt to ban Christmas, and why did they fail?
- festivals. This could be very like calendars but need not be. It would examine reasons for observing religious and secular, family and community occasions. How and why Christmas is celebrated would be one of the examples chosen
- Christmas past (in the Middle Ages, for example) and Christmas in other countries (especially the stories which are told) are other topics which enable teachers to ring the changes, so that monotonous repetition can be avoided and the season can be one when real learning takes place.

Whatever the topic, the religious education aim must be kept in mind, namely understanding, at a level suitable for the children, how Christians observe Christmas, and what it means to them.

Issues

There are matters arising which fall beyond the scope of this book, but which must be noted.

1 Should the school community *celebrate* Christmas? If it decides to, how?
2 If there is a Christmas assembly, should hymns affirming personal belief be used (e.g. 'In the Bleak Mid Winter', 'Once in Royal David's City'), or should children only be invited to sing carols such as 'The Twelve Days of Christmas' or 'I Saw Three Ships'? What is being said to non-religious parents, or those of faiths other than Christian, if this is held in a church?
3 Christmas should not be a time for moralizing against extravagance! If schools wish to use it to make collections for the local elderly or people in need, that, of course, is something that they will do whatever they read in this book, but if they wish to represent Christianity fairly they should not convey the impression that loving one's neighbour is something which Christians do only at Christmas.

Perhaps the keeping of Christmas in schools would be helped by us asking what of Passover, or one of the Muslim Eids, could we observe as a school community? What could we only learn about and observe? The issue may be of obvious importance only in schools which are multifaith in membership, but when the assumption is made that all white children are Christian it does make it difficult to teach Christianity as one would teach another religion.

Further reading

For the teacher

Books listed in the general Bibliography and Chapter 10, plus:

Celebrating Christmas, CEM, 1986.
Christmas, A Ewans, RMEP, 1982.

For the classroom

'Christmas 5–14', *Teaching RE*, Autumn 1992.
My Class at Christmas, Watts, 1986, (Key Stage 1/2).
The Nativity, Julie Vivas, Cambridge University Press, 1988 (Key Stage 1).
    Teachers will need to adapt the words from this King James Version text but the illustrations are excellent. Likewise:
Christmas, Jan Pienkowski, Heinemann, 1984.
'Christmas around the world', *Child Education*, December 1992, Scholastic Publications (Key Stage 2/3).
Gifts and the gift-bringers, Judith Lowndes, the Exploring a Theme series, CEM.

12 Christian history and the denominations

Introduction

Christian diversity

When visits to churches and clergy visitors are mentioned in INSET or curriculum courses, the guaranteed response of at least one person will be: 'Aren't we going to get into trouble with parents for not going to the parish church or inviting in the Catholic priest?'

How can we be fair to all the denominations? We can't, if being fair means visiting every church in Birmingham, not to mention a mosque, gurdwara etc. We will discuss this problem later; first, we need to have some understanding of why there are so many different Christian groups or denominations.

Diversity is the essence of Christianity. The New Testament begins with four Gospels – four portraits of Jesus, each authentic for the community for which it was written. There have been attempts to harmonize them, but today most scholars would admit that the results are not convincing. There is also evidence that the different churches in Corinth, Rome and elsewhere had their own forms of organization. Only gradually, after Constantine began to favour Christians in 313CE with his Edict of Toleration, were Christian leaders throughout the Roman Empire legally able to meet together. When they did they tried to achieve uniformity but never successfully, even after 393, when Christianity became the only legal religion in the Empire.

The early Church

From its beginnings there has been diversity in Christian belief. There were some Jewish Christians, within a few decades of Jesus' ministry, who argued that he was human, not divine, an inspired man, rather like their great prophets of the past. They could not accept the idea of God taking human form. They were known as Ebionites. There were Gentiles who found it equally difficult to believe that God could possibly inhabit such a despicable thing as the human body. Jesus was really a spiritual being who appeared to be human. He came to teach mystical knowledge which would deliver them from imprisonment in the body. People who held these kinds of views were called Gnostics.

The eastern and western churches split

The Apostles' Creed, which became the agreed teaching of the Church, was only accepted gradually – and it dates to the 3rd century, not to the times of the Apostles. It, and other creeds like it, were attempts to unite all Christians in one faith. However, there were also differences in the way that the churches appointed their leaders, who came to be called bishops. Until the time of the Emperor Constantine, at least, the Christians of Alexandria elected their own bishops without referring the matter to anyone else. Eventually, in the west, the leadership of the bishop of Rome was accepted. He was the successor of St Peter, believed to be the first bishop there. Many western bishops had been called Pope, a word which means 'Father'; now it came to be used as a special title for one person.

In 1054 the eastern church, centred on Byzantium (Constantinople, now Istanbul), and the western church split. The east had never accepted the leadership of the Pope. Culturally, eastern Christians belonged to the Greek world, which regarded Romans as barbarians. There had always really been two main expressions of Christianity. It was not surprising that a break occurred. It finally came over some words which western churches had added to another statement of belief, the Nicene Creed: 'We believe in the Holy Spirit, the Lord, the giver of life, who proceeds from the Father, *and the Son*. With Father and Son he is worshipped and glorified'. Those who objected to the addition became known as Orthodox Christians, because they kept to the statement that had been agreed at the Council of Nicea in 325. The west were the unorthodox deviants. They had changed the Apostolic Faith.

In the west, which means Europe, excluding Russia, Greece, Turkey, Romania and parts of the former Yugoslavia, Christianity remained united for the next 500 years. From time to time there were individuals or groups of people who questioned the teachings but they were dealt with fairly easily and severely. The individuals were usually intellectuals, teachers in universities. They might be convinced by argument or dismissed from their posts. At worst they could be condemned as heretics, believers in false doctrines, excommunicated (that is, refused the sacraments and put out of the Church). They then passed into the hands of the ruler who might decide to imprison them or even have them put to death. If groups of men and women opposed the teachings of the Church, that might be more serious. However, Christian monarchs usually regarded it as their duty to support the Church, so they might use their soldiers to get rid of heretics.

This relationship between Church and State worked reasonably well to their mutual benefit until the 16th century. However, there was now some feeling that the taxes paid to Rome might remain in England, Scotland, France, or Sweden, or wherever they were collected, instead of going to Italy, where they did not seem to be put to good use. Often they were used to pay for the Pope's wars or palaces. They might as well pay for the wars and palaces of the English or French monarch! There were also many other criticisms of the Church and its representatives, of monasteries which took the land of villagers to turn it into grazing for sheep, and of priests who were scarcely literate enough to read the Mass, for example. However, the successful challenge to the authority of the Pope came as a complete surprise to everyone.

Martin Luther

There was a young monk living in Germany called Martin Luther (1483–1546). He was a devout priest who was deeply concerned by the state of the Church. He had visited Rome and had been very disturbed by what he saw. There seemed to be more interest in money and luxurious living than in caring for the poor and needy. The crisis came when he was back in Germany and heard a Pope's representative selling indulgences. The Church has always had a right and duty to forgive sins. Jesus once said to his disciples:
'If you forgive anyone's sins, they stand forgiven; if you pronounce them unforgiven, they remain unforgiven.'
(John 20:23)

The Church is the successor of the first followers of Jesus. This man was selling forgiveness, so it seemed to Martin Luther. He was telling people that if they bought an indulgence, a paper granting the purchaser pardon and forgiveness, their sins would be forgiven. They could even buy such pardons on behalf of dead relatives. Some people put the preacher's words into a rhyme:
'As soon as the money in the coffer rings,
The soul from Hell's torment springs.'

The monk, Luther, was disturbed by what he saw. Poor people were being exposed to emotional blackmail, persuaded to part with the little money they had to release a child who had died in infancy, or a parent, from the torment of Hell. He had also read Paul's Letter to the Romans in the New Testament. He found the words:
'He shall gain life who is justifed through faith'
(1:17, quoting the Jewish prophet Habbakuk [2:4])

He had concluded that there was no need to pay for forgiveness; Jesus had already paid the price by his death. All that was needed was faith in Jesus. In the manner of scholars of his day he decided to seek a debate on the subject of indulgences, but church officials were in no mood to have this valuable source of income challenged. The money was needed urgently to build the new church of St Peter's in Rome. Martin Luther was summoned before one of the Pope's representatives to answer for his conduct. Realizing what this might mean, he fled instead, to a place called Wittenburg, to seek the protection of its ruler. A debate did take place eventually, but it was clear that Luther's protests were not going to be heeded. From challenging indulgences he moved on to questioning the authority of the papacy itself. The princes did not all side with the Church; many of them supported Luther, who was allowed to remain free to protest and spread his views. He and his supporters regarded themselves as reformers. They did not wish to destroy the Church but to bring it back to the faith of the Apostles, which, they believed, it had neglected. What Martin Luther began is therefore known as the Reformation. He, and those after him who have shared his ideas, are called Protestants.

Authority

At the root of the different denominations lies the issue of authority. It was the authority of the Pope which Martin Luther and others like him challenged. It is the question of authority which lies at the heart of the divisions between the different denominations. Eventually, in the west three answers evolved to the question of where this lies.

The first was traditional. Authority is vested in the Pope, the successor of the Apostle Peter, who was appointed by Jesus, who said:
'You are Peter, the Rock; and on this rock I will build my church'
(Matthew 16:18)

The second group followed the teachings of Luther and others, who came before him, but whose ideas were untimely and were crushed. They said that authority lay in scripture. Most Protestant denominations belong to this group. The Church of England (or Anglican Church), however, whilst repudiating the authority of the Pope, accepts the importance of tradition and the authority of scripture. Others also protested against the teachings of the Catholic Church but said that authority lay in the inspiration of the Holy Spirit. Of these the best known denomination is probably the Society of Friends, or Quakers. Each of the new denominations developed its own form of church organization and government; some kept bishops, others placed the emphasis upon the congregation of believers. Other denominations emerged from time to time in Britain, especially the Methodists. They were founded by John Wesley, an Anglican priest who was conscious that the Church was not reaching such people as the tin-miners of Cornwall in their villages far from existing places of worship. Later came the Salvation Army whose founder, William Booth, was a Methodist who felt that his church had lost its early concern for the poor and left it to work among them in 1861. The question of authority lay at the heart of the split of western Christianity in the 15th and 16th centuries but later divisions were for other reasons.

A characteristic of the 20th century is the ecumenical movement, co-operation between denominations in local councils of churches. In 1972 most Congregationalists and Presbyterians came together formally to create the United Reformed Church. Two obstacles stand in the way of other churches uniting. At the top the leaders cannot agree over the old issue of authority, and the Christians in the pew are often too set in their ways to join with others.

Christian denominations in the UK

Figure X shows the relationship between the main denominations found in the United Kingdom. In England they fall into four categories: the established Church; the Roman Catholic Church; the Eastern or Orthodox Church and the Free Churches (i.e. free of such requirements as the need to accept the creeds), who are also called dissenters (from their rejection of the 39 articles of the Anglican Church) or non-conformists (because they refused to conform to laws requiring everyone to be an Anglican).

Teaching suggestions

Teachers need to have a basic knowledge of the denominations and church history, including local history, which may have a tree under which John Wesley preached because the parson would not let him use the parish church, or because it couldn't hold the thousands who went to hear him. There may be a priest's hole where a Catholic family sheltered courageous men who moved about the country ministering in secret to Catholics in the reign of Elizabeth I. There may be the tomb of a Catholic saint or a memorial to Protestants who were executed by burning in the reign of Mary Tudor. The story of the Christian Church has been and still is shameful in many aspects; this should not be hidden, but the reasons are what concern Religious Education. These should be examined. The purpose is not to tell horror stories or to take sides.

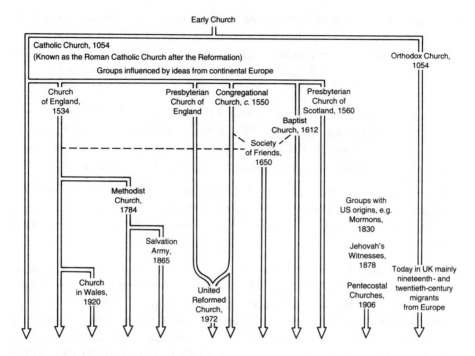

Figure I Christian denominations in the UK

NB It is difficult to separate worship and denominational distinctiveness especially at Key Stage 1 and Key Stage 2. This shouldn't concern the teacher too much. At Key Stage 1 and Key Stage 2 different ways of doing things may be noted, but not the underlying reasons or the names of denominations.

Key Stage 1

At this stage pupils should develop an awareness that churches exist. They might visit one locally and acquire a basic knowledge about it and the people who attend it, the Christian community. They could also get some idea of what children like themselves do who go to it. (See also the Key Stage 1 suggestions on worship, page 93.)

Key Stage 2

Pupils could visit two places of worship of different denominations and appearance (NB to the untrained eye Roman Catholic, Anglican and perhaps some Methodist churches look very alike). The centrality of the altar or pulpit, the presence of a font or baptistry can be used to lead into some of the differences of emphasis relating to authority. (See again Key Stage 2 worship suggestions, page 94.)

Religious customs and symbols and their meaning could be introduced, along with their stories, e.g. the cross, Easter eggs, the Christmas tree – and how many of these have been incorporated into Christianity. (Here is a link with festivals, chapters 10 and 11, which are really acts of worship.)

Links could be made with local history in the National Curriculum. For example, when Christianity came to Britain, the death of St Alban, the church in Lullingstone Roman villa, the Hinton St Mary mosaic of the head of Jesus, Iona and Lindisfarne, St Augustine at Canterbury, Thomas à Becket, the Reformation, the Salvation Army and Victorian England.

There may be local features related to these which teachers can use (e.g. the Pilgrim's Way [A272] from Winchester to Canterbury; pilgrim tracks leading to St David's cathedral; holy wells and crosses which survive in place names).

NB History and Geography may be interested in routes, where the stone came from for building the cathedral or church, but in Religious Education the importance lies in religious meaning and purpose, in sharing the joys, griefs and religious activities of the believing community not as something far distant but by entering into the time we are discussing, e.g. what stories might the children of the Hinton St Mary villa have heard? Why might the family have become Christian? What might it say about them that they had a portrayal of Jesus on the floor? If the class had been Christians would this have bothered them, and why? or how might some of the characters in the story of St Alban have reacted to his courageous death?

Or again we might think of a Celtic, Roman, Irish, Saxon or Viking family converting to Christianity, its motives, the effects of conversion, the family debate which may have occurred, the retention of old practices but with new meanings (see above). But first, we would want to look at the religions in themselves as authentic world views, not as superstitions (words which should not be used in Religious Studies). The old religions worked for many people for long periods of time. This might be Key Stage 3 work in many schools, but please note, the study of these religions is a necessary part of understanding their history. RE is really about the six principal religions found in Britain today.

Key Stage 3/Key Stage 4

At this level a deeper exploration might be made of some of the things mentioned above. The links between worship and denominational distinctiveness, for example, infant and believers' baptism, the ways it is performed and what it means; confirmation and becoming a church member.

Church organization may need to be known but should be soft-pedalled. It can be boring and is largely irrelevant to the concerns of our pupils and to understanding the Church as the people of God. If we consider it important that does not mean that pupils will. The chart provided above and a hand-out on terms such as bishop, priest, elder, deacon and minister might well be enough.

Two sensitive areas for study in the National History Curriculum at Key Stage 3 are the Crusades and the Holocaust.

The Crusades

These wars were fought for a variety of motives. It is important that pupils should be aware of the religious dimensions, and here there is an opportunity for History and RE to combine. If we look back to the list of concepts (see page 57) we find faith, worship, prayer, ritual, commitment and belonging to a faith community mentioned. All are important in teaching about the Crusades.

Faith It was belief that the holy places in Palestine should be under Christian control that motivated some Christians. Their faith was sometimes exploited by stories which were told about Muslims defiling them. Honesty requires teachers to tell this side of the story, as well as achievements by Christian heroes.

Worship and ritual These might come together in the examination of pilgrim journeys to Christian sites in Palestine or on the way. Their significance for Christians would link with:

Commitment The zeal of many Christians who went on the Crusades, inspired by their belief that they were doing God's will. This is perhaps the concept most central to the study of this theme.

Belonging to a faith community Those who could not make the journey often helped those who went by giving money and praying for them. Western Europe may never have had a stronger sense of Christian unity at any other time in its history.

Prayer Some prayers used by Crusaders or for their success might be studied.

The Crusades provide the RE teacher with a good opportunity to examine the essence of Christianity, and the essence of the Crusades, and to help pupils study the evidence without prejudice.

Anti-semitism was a Christian, not a Muslim, feature of the Crusades which should be introduced in this theme but studied in fuller depth in the Holocaust.

The Holocaust

History may look at the rise of Hitler and reasons for his anti-Jewish policy. RE must go back not only to Martin Luther but to the New Testament. It must consider the attitude to Jews found in John's Gospel and the Synoptics. Jews place the blame for the Holocaust firmly upon Christianity, asserting that its modern origins lie in its foundation document, the New Testament, and pointing out that the perpetrators of the Holocaust were baptized Christians. Christians, of course, are likely to make the riposte that the Nazis were not really Christians.

RE lessons might focus on such biblical passages as:

- the passion and crucifixion accounts in the Gospels – where do they apportion blame?
- Matthew 27:25, which was used as an excuse to 'punish' Jews on God's behalf for the crucifixion
- John 8:31–59, perhaps. This is a difficult and unpleasant passage which demonstrates that in the place where the Gospel was written Jews and the followers of Jesus had gone their separate ways with the usual bitterness that a broken relationship brings.

Of course, attention must be given to the Christians who opposed Hitler and the Nazis. (*Dying We Live*, listed in Further reading, contains the final messages and records of some Christians who defied Hitler. Dietrich Bonhoeffer is a good case study to examine.)

Since 1945 churches have condemned anti-semitism. Most notable was the document *Nostra Aetate*, produced by the Roman Catholic Church in 1965, which made three points: Christians come from the stock of Judaism; Christians owe a debt to Judaism; Jesus should be a reason for Jewish–Christian reconciliation, not hostility.

This matter is discussed in greater detail in the Issues section at the end of Chapter 7.

Finally, whilst it was Christians who attempted to blame the Jews as a race for the crucifixion, racism extends far beyond Christianity. The teacher must decide whether to confine this Key Stage 3 study to the Holocaust, leaving Christianity and racism till later, or to cover everything now. We might advise delay. Racism is not confined to hatred of Jews, nor is it inspired only by religion; in fact the world's religions are united in denouncing it.

Key Stage 4

Christian beliefs and reflection on how different Christians have and do respond to them, e.g. the resurrection of the body, eternal (not everlasting) life, could be introduced. As far as possible the issues of belief should reflect the *actual* heated debates which took place and led to the need for a creed, a canon of scripture, and divisions – but remember that the situation today is that the churches are agreed on most doctrines; the biggest differences may exist between charismatic Roman Catholics or Anglicans who feel comfortable with charismatic Baptists, and more staid Catholics and Baptists, who find charismatic worship a threat!

Inter-denominational strife has been a feature of Christianity from pre-Reformation times. There is a case for letting sleeping dogs lie. After all, RE should be about the here and now, living religion, as far as possible. If, however, we feel the need to enter the historical period of the Scottish Covenanters, the Reformation or the Restoration, then it should be by means of case studies of sincere men and women, not the prelates or politicians, who were often time-servers. Using imagination and empathy, we should be able to know why good people on both sides were willing to risk everything for their convictions.

Issues

There are four issues:

- we should decide how far we need to go into denominationalism. Probably not far. If we do, we should keep it light, brief and, as has already been suggested, related to people like St Thomas More or William Tyndale, so that it is humanized. These could be two good Reformation case studies
- we should maintain some distinction between worship and denominations but at Key Stage 3 in ideas of baptism and Key Stage 4 in such things as interpretations of the eucharist and the reasons underlying them. If we do, the necessary features should emerge
- we should try to look at the religious story of the Church, rather than the history of the denominations, and do it, as suggested above, through the lives of Christians and the beliefs which inspired them
- we should be honest in evaluating the actions of Christians but we should help our pupils to bear in mind that they were people of their time and that sincere motives can and do warp human conduct.

Further reading

For the teacher

A Report on Afro-Caribbean Christianity in Britain, V Howard, University of Leeds Dept of Religious Studies, 1987.

The Orthodox Church, Timothy Ware, Mowbray, 1967.
The Orthodox Church, Timothy Ware, Penguin, 1963.

For the classroom

An Ebony Cross, I Smith and W Green, Marshall Pickering, 1989. Contains case study material useful at Key Stage 3/4.
Living in Harmony – The Story of Sybil Phoenix, John Newbury, RMEP, 1985. Mrs Phoenix is a well-known British black Christian (Key Stage 2/3).
Medieval Islam, P Bartley and H Bourdillon, Hodder and Stoughton, 1993.
The Crusades, P Mantin and R Pulley, Hodder and Stoughton, 1993 (Key Stage 3/4).
The Islamic World, P Mantin and R Mantin, CUP, 1993.

Teachers including the Holocaust or Crusades in RE might use the following:
Dying We Live, eds. H Gollwitzer, K Kuhn and R Schneider, Harvill Press, 1956. The last letters or observers' memories of executed opponents of Hitler, ranging from a farm boy to aristocrats and theologians (Key Stage 3 selectively, Key Stage 4 and upwards).
Smoke and Ashes, OUP, 1991 (Key Stage 3). A study of the Holocaust for slightly older pupils.*
The Number on my Grandfather's Arm, 1987 (Key Stage 2). A moving story which will help children understand the Holocaust.*

Video

Dear Kitty. 27 minutes. Children witness the Holocaust (Key Stage 2).*
ITV Believe it or Not series, CV0141, CV0142, CV0143, CV0144, Articles of Faith. Each video contains several programmes, not all on Christianity. Subjects include confirmation, Salvation Army, Caribbean Roman Catholic and Pentecostal (Key Stage 2/3).
The Black Pentecostal Experience, ILEA. Available from Educational Media, 235 Imperial Drive, Rayners Lane, Harrow, Middlesex HA2 7HE.
The Holocaust and Yad Vashem, 30 minutes. Takes the viewer through the sequence of events which led to the Holocaust and then into its course (Key Stage 4 and upwards).

(*Can be obtained from the Jewish Education Bureau; see Appendix 2.)

13 Christian ethics

Introduction

All religions provide guidance or rules governing personal and social conduct. This is as true of Christianity as any other. Jesus built upon his Jewish heritage in this respect. Distinctive aspects of his teaching occur in many places, as we shall see, but Christians would point to the Sermon on the Mount more than any other block of teaching. It is to be found in Matthew's Gospel, chapters 5 to 7. (In Luke's Gospel much of it is found in chapter 6, but some is used elsewhere. Matthew's material is the most convenient to study, as well as the best known.) Jesus makes two points relevant to our discussion. First he says:

'Do not think that I have come to destroy the Law and the prophets; I have not come to destroy but to fulfil. Truly, I tell you, till heaven and earth pass away, not an iota, not a dot, will pass from the Law until all is accomplished.'

(Matthew 5:18–19)

The Law was, of course, the ethical teaching of the Jewish Torah.

Secondly, Jesus quotes passages from the Torah and adds his own comments; for example:

'You have heard that it was said, "An eye for an eye and a tooth for a tooth." But I say to you, Do not resist one who is evil. But if anyone strikes you on the right cheek, turn to him the other also; and if anyone sue you and take away your coat, let him have your cloak as well; and if anyone forces you to go with him one mile, go with him two.'

(This was apparently what a member of the occupying Roman forces could require of people they had conquered.)

(Matthew 5:38–42)

'I' in this passage and others like it is a significant little word. It may suggest that he, Jesus is claiming to be the true interpreter of the Torah. All sages, Jewish religious teachers, explained what the Torah meant to their disciples. Christians claim that Jesus was giving the definitive explanation and placing himself on a par with the giver of the Torah, God. Here is the difference between Jesus and the Jewish prophets, who also interpreted the Torah to the people of their own day. Another difference is the claim that the ethical teachings of Jesus are timeless, not related to particular circumstances, as those of the prophets sometimes were. What Jesus shared with them was the importance he attached to the Torah and the demands he made upon his followers. Ethics were not something to be taken lightly. Some Christians have even described the Sermon on the Mount as setting impossible standards. No so-called Christian country has ever based its legislation upon them, though some communities have done from time to time.

Christian ethics are based on principles, not precise regulations; after all, these already existed in the 613 Jewish commandments, many of which Jesus and the disciples kept. For example, in Acts chapter 10 Peter states that forbidden food had never touched his mouth. When people came to Jesus for rules for living it is interesting to find that he often told a story (a parable; see page 83) which required the questioners to do some thinking for themselves. For example, when a group of scribes and Pharisees, fellow teachers of the Torah, criticized Jesus for mixing with Jews who were tax collectors and sinners, people who were slack in observing the Torah, he told them what is known as the parable of the Lost Son (Luke 15:11–32). You might like to read the parable before looking at the rest of this section.

The story is not explicitly explained and the horrible picture of the younger son working among pigs and eating their food may be lost to some extent upon a non-Jewish audience, but two contrasting features of it come out clearly. First, there is the father, longing for the son to return and greeting him without rubbing in his shortcomings. Then there is the older son, who is understandably angry. In its original setting it is not difficult to work out the meaning: that the father is God, that the younger son represents the Torah-neglecting tax collectors and sinners, and that the older son speaks for the scribes and Pharisees. But if Jesus had spelled it out, what would it mean today, when most people who listen to it are not Jews? Its power lies in its ability to challenge racist or class-conscious Christians, or simply families in which there is jealousy today or at any time.

It is clear that the teachings of Jesus stressed love, mercy and forgiveness. 'Love your neighbour as yourself' (Leviticus 19:18) was the basis of the Torah and Jesus' teaching alike (Luke 10:27–8). When the Church decided to admit non-Jews into membership it therefore laid rules upon them which were based on this injunction. In a letter to all the churches the Apostles said that Christians should abstain from meat offered to idols, from meat still containing blood, from anything which had been strangled (and would thus still contain blood), and from fornication. The principle was that Jewish and Gentile Christians should express their love for one another in practice. Similarly, St Paul could write:
'Baptized into union with him, you have all put on Christ as a garment. There is no such thing as Jew and Greek, slave and freeman, male and

female: for you are all one person in Christ Jesus.'
(Galatians 3:27–8)

This was not understood to mean that Christians should not own slaves, but there are several passages in the New Testament which say that they should be well-treated. Gradually, Christians came to believe that the 'love your neighbour' principle meant the rejection of slavery and its kindred practice of apartheid in South Africa. Slowly racism is being condemned for the same reason, but by no means all Christians would extend it to gender-equality, and many who do would exempt the priesthood from being covered by the statement that in Christ there is no such thing as male and female. Prison reform, capital punishment and pacifism are other areas where Christians debate among themselves how the principles of love, mercy and forgiveness should be carried out in practice, especially the words of Jesus:
'Love your enemies.'
(Matthew 5:44, Luke 6:27, 35)

Teaching suggestions

Key Stage 1

Children could be introduced to some stories which illustrate Christian ethical teaching. These would include men as well as women, of a variety of races, with the emphasis being upon people living today. For example, Christian Aid and CAFOD workers and Mother Theresa. These should be taught as exemplars of Jesus' teaching, not as moral examples which children are encouraged to follow. Few stories from the New Testament would seem suitable at this stage. Zacchaeus, the forgiven tax collector (Luke 19:1–10) can be used much more meaningfully at Key Stage 2.

Key Stage 2

The forgiveness of Peter (John 21) is an important part of the resurrection accounts, and also, perhaps, the appearance to Doubting Thomas, (John 20:26–30), though this might benefit from being left to Key Stage 3.

Further examples of Christians might be used – not always the great and the good, but members of the Salvation Army or local church groups which help the homeless. Some of them might be able to find time to come to school to describe their work.

Key Stage 3

Jesus' words as he was being crucified, 'Father, forgive them, they do not know what they are doing' (Luke 23:34) might be a subject for reflection.

Used earlier, it might demonstrate weakness, not strength, to macho boys. The forgiveness of Paul the persecutor might also be something that can be understood. The woman who had committed adultery (John 7:53–8:11) and the incident in Luke 7:36–50 are other classic accounts of Jesus forgiving people. By this time many of the parables of Jesus could be used, as well as such signs of the Kingdom as the forgiveness of the paralytic man (Mark 2:1–12) and the words which Jesus used to proclaim his mission (Luke 4:16–30).

St Francis, and the women who became missionaries to the Acua tribal South Americans who had earlier killed their husbands, are further examples in the ongoing story of Christians who have followed the precepts of Jesus. Local Christian care agencies might again be approached for speakers. The appropriateness or extent to which schools or classes might become involved in their work is for them to consider.

Some teachers might be concerned that the picture is being presented in such a way that children may conclude that only Christians care. At Key Stage 3 and Key Stage 4, in particular, it should be possible to bring in other people whose motivation is not religious, to explain what they do and why. In earlier key stages in areas such as Wolverhampton, where faiths worked together very closely to provide relief for Bosnian refugees, Muslims or Sikhs who helped might visit the school. There are Jewish care agencies whose local members might be prepared to speak about their work. However, this is a book on teaching Christianity and it is to that task that we must mainly confine ourselves.

The Lord's Supper/eucharist/mass has a strong ethical element to it. This should not be surprising, as it seems to characterize meal-sharing in many religions. Its spiritual significance is, of course, paramount but when the first Christians met together it is said that:
'They all kept up their daily attendance at the Temple, and, breaking bread in their homes, they shared their meals with unaffected joy.'
(Acts 2:46)

'Breaking of bread' was a phrase frequently used in reference to what became Holy Communion. The emphasis was upon corporate unity and solidarity, especially in the dangerous months following the death of their leader and in the periods of persecution which they faced during the next three centuries. However, converts did not easily set aside their old attitudes. St Paul had to take the Christians of Corinth to task for turning the Lord's Supper into a meal which perpetuated class divisions rather than unity. In 1 Corinthians 11 he writes: 'When you meet as a congregation, it is not the Lord's Supper that you eat; when it comes to eating, each of you takes his own supper, one goes hungry and another one has too much to drink. Have you no homes of your own to eat and drink in? Or are you so contemptuous of the church of God that you shame its poorer members?'

The rich, it seems, were bringing their Fortnum and Mason hampers while the poor, at the other side of the meeting places, fed on the scraps which they could save to bring to the meal, which was actually called an agapé, a love feast! One reason for the symbolic drop of wine and wafer or small piece of bread which Christians eat today in a eucharist is the prevention of the class-consciousness which Paul encountered. Many Christians use one cup and break one loaf of bread, which is passed around the group as a way of demonstrating their common fellowship. In India there have been cases of brahmin converts having to be given the elements of bread and wine before Christians of lower caste to avoid ritual pollution. Old traditions die hard. But before anyone becomes judgemental, it should be noted that officially Roman Catholics cannot open up the mass to members of other Christian churches.

Key Stage 4

With sensitivity, the sacrament of Holy Communion provides much scope for study, not only as a central feature of Christian worship but as an aspect of Christian ethics.

The Church, the ecclesia, the men and women who felt called to be the body of Christ, also provides material for ethical study, from the disputes of the disciples through to the ecumenical movement of modern times and the communities which have been formed since the first members in Jerusalem: '...agreed to hold every thing in common: they began to sell their property and possessions and distribute to everyone according to his need.'
(Act 2:44–5)

Followers of Charles de Foucauld exist as communities, though often going about their daily lives as lay men and women in society, owning their own homes and earning their livings in the kinds of jobs that the rest of us do, but meeting frequently and working as a community spiritually and in helping the homeless or drug-affected. L'Arche, Communities of the Ark, whose origins go back to 1963, cares for the handicapped, but we use the word cautiously, recognizing a sentence in its charter which reads: 'The person with a handicap is a complete human being and as such has the rights of every human being.'

These communities, as well as the more traditional ones, might provide a focus in studying Christian ethics at Key Stages 3 and 4. It is for the teacher to decide whether to use them in exploring what 'Church' means as well, or to distinguish between ethics and the Church. They belong together, of course, but sometimes distinctions are necessary for educational reasons. (The use of visitors in RE is discussed on page 48)

Christian ethics have to do with genetic engineering, care for the elderly, the family, abortion, in fact the whole of life, as well as so-called simple matters of right and wrong. These issues provide almost endless opportunities for study from Key Stage 4 onwards, but we would suggest that there are three requirements which should be borne in mind:

1 particular aspects should always be studied in the context of Christian world views. As we have said earlier, Christian ethics are based on Christian beliefs. Unless these are understood first, the specific Christian dimensions of, say, the punishment of criminals cannot be discussed meaningfully

2 the study should be based on evidence and information, not hand-me-down parental views, even if they may be those of a priest. The priest may not be impartial (most classroom discussions on ethics in the past seem to have been at the level of sharing uninformed opinions)

3 the purpose of the exploration is to understand, not to impose a particular view or even require pupils to make up their minds about the topic.

Two books which teachers might find helpful are *Ethics and Religions*, J Rankin, A Brown and P Gateshill, Longman, 1991 and *Moral Issues in Six Religions*, ed. W Owen Cole, Heinemann Educational, 1991. *Contemporary Moral Issues*, J Jenkins, Heinemann Educational, 1989 and 1992, is also recommended, but does not set ethics in the context of one particular world view. See also Jenkins' *Introducing Moral Issues*, Heinemann Educational, 1994. The sections on Christianity in the other two books are explicitly Christian.

Issues

There are at least four issues which we have to consider when we teach Christian ethics. They are:

• the distinction between teaching Christian ethics and moral education. In this chapter we are concerned with helping children to understand the nature of Christian ethics in the same way that, in a different context, we would be examining Muslim or Humanist ethics. Our work would contribute to pupils' understanding of ethics but would not be aimed specifically at teaching them to distinguish right from wrong. Moral education has a much broader remit than Religious Education

• the recognition that values are derived from beliefs. This is a major reason why moral education and religious education cannot be synonymous. 'Love your enemies' is a command that calls for some response from those who dare to call themselves Christians. It can be ignored by any groups or individuals for whom love of enemies is not a belief

- the recognition that Christian ethics are dynamic. Who knows, one day Christians might admit that the youngster who brings the paper at 7am in time for them to scan it over breakfast is being exploited just as much as the migrant workers who serve as waiters and cleaners in our exclusive hotels. If Christians were to comment on such matters, would they simply be becoming conscientiously objectionable and unrealistic?

- care in handling Jewish ethics in the Christian ethical context. It is very easy to damn Judaism as legalistic and commend Christian ethics as based upon the principle of love of neighbours. Only by ignoring great chunks of penal history or arguing that the governments which accepted slavery, children working in mines or transportation to Australia for poaching were not inspired by Christian principles can this claim be made. It depends, too, on an ignorance of Judaism – despite the fact that some of the stories we use may be from the Old Testament. Somehow we forget that these were Jewish before Christians began to use them, and that they remain Jewish still.

A Pharisee asked a man who wanted to be his disciple what he would do if someone had an accident on the Sabbath. 'Consult the Torah' was the reply. 'That would do no good,' said the Pharisee. 'By the time you had done that the poor man would be dead. Go and do something else!'

The classic example of the need for sensitivity is with regard to the use of the phrase 'an eye for an eye and a tooth for a tooth'. This occurs in Exodus 21:24. The Jewish interpretation of the words is that they mean that compensation should be paid equivalent to the loss sustained and that unlimited retribution is forbidden. In fact, the rabbis based compensation of such factors as pain suffered, the effect on looks, loss of earnings, sex, and age, things insurers and industrial tribunals have started to take into account only in recent times. It might also be noted that at its foundation Israel rejected capital punishment, because it was contrary to the consensus of scripture. Many Israelis disapproved when it passed a law permitting the execution of Adolf Eichmann.

Further reading

For the teacher

Christian Ethics in a Secular World, R Gill, Clark, 1991.
Exploring a Theme: the Environment, CEM. Good ideas for teaching about environmental issues in the primary school.
Groundwork of Christian Ethics, R G Jones, Epworth, 1984.

For the classroom

Contemporary Moral Issues, J Jenkins, Heinemann Educational, 1989 and 1992.
Ethics and Religions, J Rankin, A Brown and P Gateshill, Longman, 1991.
Introducing Moral Issues, J Jenkins, Heinemann Educational, 1994.
Moral Issues in Six Religions, ed. W Owen Cole, Heinemann Educational, 1991.

14 The diversity and dynamic of Christianity

Introduction

Institutions and individuals are constantly changing. Your school is not the same it was even 10 years ago, not only because of the turnover of staff and pupils and the National Curriculum, but also as a result of changing pupil-teacher relationships ansd social developments. Families and nations change, too, and so do human beings. If they don't they die, because they are living organisms. One dynamic response is to try to return to what we perceive the past to have been like, but each of us has our own memory of this. It is rather like attempting to produce Handel's *Messiah* using original instruments and careful research to capture the authenticity of two centuries ago. It is fascinating, but can we be certain that it sounds like the version which the audience first heard in Dublin? After all, since then we have heard Verdi, Elgar, Mahler and Stravinsky. Can modern performers erase them totally from their minds? At the other extreme are the so-called trendy Shakespeare productions in modern dress. So it is with religion. There are those who believe that there is a given, a revelation, a beacon to which the seeker must come. They usually present this in a particular way of understanding the Bible or a 'traditionalist' concept of the Church. There are others who argue that changes are responses to the prompting of the Holy Spirit. In Religious Education we are not required to take sides, in fact, unless we are Christians it is an impertinence to do so, rather like intruding upon a family quarrel – or a family wedding – when we are neither friends nor relatives. So we must beware of asking the class whether they think modern forms of worship are a good thing or not, or whether it makes any sense to pray in the late 20th century, or whether Christians should support abortion. What we can try to help children to understand is the kinds of issues which concern Christians, the varied responses they make, and the reasons for them. In this chapter we look at three areas: attitudes to other races and religions, liberation theology, and the place of women. Reference is made to modern ethical concerns elsewhere (see page 127).

These are all matters for detailed study at Key Stage 4 and later, but a beginning can and must be made earlier because most of them impinge upon other aspects of Christianity, which children will encounter even at Key

Stage 1. To take race and religion as an example, in many classes there will be black, Asian or Chinese children, some of them Christian some of them of other religions. To suggest, by the Christian examples chosen and the exclusive portrayal of Jesus as white (and Judas sometimes as dark-skinned), that Christianity should be equated with whiteness is to endorse the European stereotype in the face of the fact that white Christians form a minority in the world population, and Jesus was not Caucasian. It also sidelines Christians of other skin-colours, which, it must be admitted, is often still done in Britain.

To return to the wider issues, however, a major assertion made in the New Testament is that Jesus was a dynamic personality who challenged the tired traditions of his heritage. The Church, called the New Israel, burst out of the old wine skins because they were not flexible enough to contain it (Matthew 9:17). This is the real meaning of the story of the wedding at Cana in John's Gospel, chapter 2. Diversity and adaptability lay at the heart of the new religion which, though Jesus only seems to have preached to his fellow Jews, was able, a few years later, to accept Gentiles into membership. The existence of four Gospels, each very different from, though also similar to the others, is evidence of an initial diversity which resulted from the Church's dynamism. Attitudes to other religions, liberation theology, and the place of women in Christianity are important aspects of modern contemporary Christianity where diverstiy and dynamism can be seen. They will be considered in some detail later in this chapter.

Teaching suggestions

Key Stage 1

When we use the two stories of the birth of Jesus, for example, or take children to visit churches, we might encourage them to think and observe for themselves and realize that there are different ways of looking at things, expressing ideas and beliefs and understanding them. If we are teaching in a neighbourhood where there is an old church and a modern one built on very different principles, we might be able to visit both and notice the differences. Representations of Jesus in stained glass windows or on Christmas cards may also differ.

Key Stage 2

It should be possible to try to discover some of the reasons for differences in stories, pictures and places. (Some Key Stage 1 children may be able to do this, of course.)

Key Stage 3

Theological and social explanations could be explored and attempts made to empathize with those who welcome change and those who were dismayed by it. As always in Religious Studies, the purpose is to understand, not to take sides.

We have already seen how a parable can be understood in various ways, depending on the circumstances (see pages 35–6). This is another way of helping children to recognize diversity from the very beginning of their religious education.

Key Stage 4

Diversity and dynamism should be explicit in almost every facet of our teaching. The complexity of Christian beliefs, practices and values are of the essence of Christianity. They should, therefore, be taught not grudgingly or apologetically, but positively.

Christianity and other religions

The Sunderland Agreed Syllabus of 1944 contains an essay entitled 'A Comparative Study of the Religions of the World' (pages 84–9 of the second edition, 1956). It begins with an outline of the history of Hebrew religion as it is contained in the Bible, then outlines the Greek philosophical tradition, the teachings of Confucius and the Buddha, followed by the 'gross polytheism' which is Hinduism, and the religion of Islam. It concludes with these words: 'Whatever is good in these religions in the conception of the character of God and of man's moral duties is found unified and elevated in the Christian religion' (page 88).

The essay is interesting for many reasons, not least for the fact that there were people who thought in 1944 that 15- and 16-year-olds might study world religions, albeit from the position of the Christian apologetic. It might repay the scrutiny of teachers undertaking research. However, its approach would be unlawful in maintained non-denominational schools in the late 20th century and unwise in denominational schools, many of which would disapprove of it. There is universal agreement among RE teachers, supported in documents related to the 1993 Act, for example Circular 1/94, that religions other than Christianity are to be taught in our schools and that the purpose must be one of understanding. The Circular speaks of 'the rigorous study of different faiths' (paragraph 9, page 10). The same paragraph also states that teachers 'have a role in promoting respect for and understanding of those with different beliefs and practices from their own'.

There is clearly no place for the subtle methods which teachers can use to put down opinions, ideas and beliefs with which they disagree, whether they be religious or political, encountered in Religious Education, History, Social Geography or Literature. Where students are sophisticated enough the teacher should realize that the methods used to undermine one religion are capable of being turned on any faith. Occasionally, preachers may encourage congregations to learn about the various religions which are part of British society, saying: 'It is important that we understand our neighbours, but you should remember that they are searching for the truth. God has revealed it to us in Jesus'. Let us be clear that this is a statement of belief. There seems to be no evidence that Christians can produce to make it a factually provable statement, any more than other faiths can provide objectively verifiable proofs for their beliefs. The Religious Education which we advocate should enable children to recognize that these are faith statements, if teachers or believers ever make them, and understand why they make them and what they mean by them.

We live in a multi-religious Britain, which is part of a pluralistic world. It would be foolish and wrong to deny children access to the world heritage which most of us discovered as adults and which some readers may not yet have encountered except through the growing number of TV programmes on dance, art, cookery, clothing and music, as well as fictional dramas and religious documentaries. We do not know what the world of our children will be like but we can be certain that it will be one in which they become aware of other cultures before they leave primary school, however Christian the Religious Education syllabus of the school and LEA might be. Our task is to help them to understand the world as it is. In the context of this book it is that of helping them to understand what attitudes Christians can have towards other religions and how they make sense of particular issues.

To take the general issue first: what attitudes do Christians have towards other religions?

Possible attitudes to religions other than one's own

1 'My religion is true: the rest are false.' There are many Christians who hold this view. It is usually linked with a literal acceptance of the words of Jesus: 'I am the way, the truth and the life; no one comes to the Father except by me' (John 14:6).

   For some Christians it causes such issues to be raised as where the spirituality which they find in other people comes from, and whether God can be so narrowly prescriptive.

2 'All earlier religions are ways provided by God to prepare the way for the coming of Jesus.' This is the traditional Christian view of Judaism, as we

have seen (see page 76). It might be extended to Hinduism, Islam and Sikhism or tribal religions. Even religions which came later than Christianity historically could be ways in which God has prepared the ground for the Gospel. In Athens St Paul saw an altar dedicated to The Unknown God and said, in effect:

'I am here to tell you about him'

(Acts 17:23)

Christians who hold this view, which gives some worth to other religions, might point out that in John's Gospel Jesus is called the logos, a Greek term meaning the eternal word of God. So they might explain John 14:6 as 'No one comes to the Father unless the logos brings them' – adding that the logos is at work in other religions. They are, however, preparations for the Gospel at best. In the end everyone will acknowledge Jesus as Lord.

3 'Christianity is from God; the rest are human searches.' Many Christians accept this idea. They would claim that everyone is religious at heart. The impulse to search is natural. Eventually it will be satisfied when people accept the way provided by God in Jesus.

4 'All paths lead to God.' Most Christians would utterly reject this notion. It would appear to make the ministry of Jesus, and especially his death, meaningless. It also suggests that the movement is *towards* God rather than initiated *by* God. Christians might well want to enter the caveat that any religion which they might accept as leading to God would have to preach a high code of personal morality as well as being monotheistic. The place of Hinduism might trouble some of them until they come to know it at first hand and discover that essentially it is not idolatrous and polytheistic.

5 'In different environments God becomes manifest in different ways.' Some Christians might look favourably upon this as an explanation for the existence of other religions – the logos takes different forms – but they would want to maintain the universality and finality of the Gospel. They would also suggest that it is only some paths which might be provided by God, those which, like Christianity, are monotheistic and ethical. The belief that Jesus is the eternal Word of God, the so-called logos doctrine of Christianity, might allow some place for this view.

Readers who are Christians may wish to consider which of these positions, if any, they hold and, with them, the whole question of what believers mean when they say that their religion is true. The problem for Christians is that of squaring their commitment to Christ and their belief in his uniqueness with the persistence of other religions which have not capitulated to the Christian mission, and also with the deep spirituality which those who know Muslims, Sikhs, Jews and others, including members of tribal religions, find in them. To ignore these facts or dismiss them simplistically is not possible in our global village.

There are also particular areas to be studied, regardless of personal belief. For example, an awareness of the religion of Islam leads to the discovery that the two religions differ in their statements, as well as their beliefs, about Jesus. The Qur'an says explicitly that Jesus is not God's son and that he was not crucified. There are other less significant differences in the use of generally similar material which invite an understanding of why the Bible and Qur'an differ from the Muslim and Christian viewpoints. Reconciling the positions is a long way off, if it can ever be achieved. The teacher of Year 9 is obviously not expected to do this, but should be able to explore the issue beyond the point of saying that Muhammad (peace be upon him) was simply ill-informed by a heretical Christian monk, or deliberately got it wrong! The reaction to the Muslim child who says: 'We don't believe that Jesus died' will be awaited eagerly by her and by Christian children in the class. The teacher who has just taught one of the Gospel stories of the crucifixion could feel threatened unless she was aware of the Islamic belief – especially if she was explicitly using the 'we believe' approach and not 'Christians believe'! The teacher has to accept and endorse the differing beliefs which Christians and Muslims, and Jews as well, have about Jesus: not easy, perhaps, for committed Christians, unless they can come to terms with the approach outlined in Part 1 of this book.

The Judaism and Christianity relationship has already been discussed (see pages 76–8). There is nothing to add here. Teachers who are Christians have been brought up to believe that the Old Testament necessarily and obviously prepares the way for Jesus. It may take something of an intellectual and emotional struggle to see the prophets in a Jewish light, turning people to the Torah, not looking towards Jesus, and to accept that the passages used in Handel's *Messiah* or the Service of Nine Lessons and Carols are capable of another valid interpretation. It is possible that we can study the Jewish concept of messiahship in a course on Judaism and never address the fact that it differs radically from the Christian at any point in the syllabus. This allows pupils to make of it what they will or just ignore the contradiction, as the uncommitted student may. It might give more clarity to our teaching to examine the different concepts together only after they have been studied separately – the Jewish first, of course. Without it the Christian makes no sense; the very word is meaningless, as 'Christ' is to most people nowadays.

Is Jesus a manifestation of God in the same way that Krishna or Rama are of Vishnu? Do Hindus worship idols? (Do Roman Catholics, for that matter?) These are questions which arise for some Christians from studying Hinduism. Teachers might read *What is Idolatry?* by Roger Hooker, a CMS missionary for many years, during which time he also studied Hinduism and Sanskrit.

In the last few paragraphs we have, of course, been discussing inter-religious encounter or dialogue. We would suggest that this is a subject that should feature explicitly in Religious Education at Key Stage 4 and beyond, as it does as yet in only a few syllabuses. For many years it must have been taking place in the minds of thoughtful students of whatever faith and often it has been the subject of out-of-class conversations between young people of different religions. Acquiring the skills to undertake the exercise properly should be part of the Religious Studies course. Real dialogue is only possible among believers; this is when the questions of truth bite, but understanding what is meant by the Muslim belief that Christians worship three gods, for example, is a matter that anyone can engage in, and it has been known to sharpen thinking about the concept of the Trinity. (Incidentally, when do we use upper case and when lower for the 'g' in god? A Key Stage 3 or Key Stage 4 matter for exploration?)

Teaching suggestions

What we have been discussing in this section is mostly for exploration at Key Stage 4 and beyond. It should not be confined to multi-religious schools, though such issues come alive when Sikh, Muslim and Christian 16-year-olds together examine the different beliefs which they, and pupils who have no religious beliefs, hold.

Key Stage 1

The School Curriculum and Assessment Authority (SCAA) model syllabuses, following the approach of many Agreed Syllabuses, encourage the teaching of other religions as well as Christianity. This should be done in a positive and interesting manner, making use of artefacts and opportunities for visits and visitors and stories supported by good pictures and videos. The aim, in mono-religious schools, is to enable children to become aware of other religions and to accept their existence.

Key Stage 2

A discussion of the Romans, the Vikings and their beliefs about God and creation has been known to act as a catalyst for exploring the teachings of different religions and the theories of science. While we would say that Key Stage 4 is where the subject should appear on the syllabus, when children have had an opportunity to examine separately the beliefs of different religions, we have to recognize, as always, that pupils do not always approach learning in the tidy, sequential way that we as teachers might desire, and that in the hands of skilful teachers they may arise at almost any time.

This awareness of religious pluralism can be extended as more understanding of Jesus, the Bible, worship, and the Christian festivals are accompanied by the separate teaching of similar aspects of one or more other religions. Properly done, this can enhance the understanding of Christianity as well as of the other religions.

Key Stages 3 and 4

This enhancement can be even more profitable. Jesus in the Bible and Qur'an and the recognition that Jesus is to Christianity what the Qur'an, not Muhammad (pbuh), is to Islam, is capable of being explored at a fairly simple level. However, the interaction of religions and matters of dialogue, areas which all students should study today, are best left until the final year of compulsory education when the knowledge necessary for such work and the maturity have been provided and developed. Topics such as the Crusades and Holocaust (see pages 121–2) necessitate the study of Islam and Judaism respectively alongside Christianity.

The work of Christian missionaries today as well as in the past should include a sensitive examination of the religions they encountered, otherwise children are invited to conclude that they took religion into a spiritual vacuum. The religion of the Vikings served them well for a long time. Modern missionaries are learning from Hindus and the teachings of the traditional religions of Africa.

Liberation theology

Church and State

The relationship between Christianity and the State has been an issue ever since Christianity began. Jesus lived and died against the background of great political upheaval and speculation. The early Christians were persecuted by the Roman Empire primarily because they were considered a *political* threat. Eventually, however, Christianity became the state religion of the Roman Empire, largely due to the influence of the Emperor Constantine (306–337CE). The strong ties between Church and State which began then have been an important feature of the development of Christianity ever since, especially in the West. It is a remarkable paradox that the religious movement which worshipped a saviour killed by means of the torture reserved for political rebels, and which was persecuted for refusing to join the army or offer incense to the Emperor, developed into the state religion and adapted many features of the Emperor cult in its worship and organization. This tension between Christianity as the radical, 'counter-cultural' charismatic movement and Christianity as the authoritarian, hierarchical representative of the State is one of the important factors in the diversity and dynamic of the Christian tradition and its history.

Christianity and politics

In the 20th century, the issues surrounding Christianity's relationship with politics have emerged most obviously in the debate surrounding liberation theology. This particular movement is understood to have begun in Latin America, but similar movements can be seen in Africa, especially South Africa, throughout the so-called Third World and also among black Christians in America. The ideas of liberation theology have also affected church leaders in Great Britain. David Sheppard, the Anglican Bishop of Liverpool, wrote a book, *Bias towards the Poor*, in which he applied the approach of the liberation theologian to Great Britain.

The term 'liberation theology' was first used by Latin American theologians in the late '60s and early '70s. The 1968 Conference of Latin American Bishops, held in Medellin, Colombia, is often seen as the historical starting point of this movement. Then in 1971 the Peruvian priest and theologian Gustavo Gutierrez published what is now considered the classic work – *A Theology of Liberation*. The ideas he presented reflected a movement which was emerging throughout Latin America, and many other writers developed these ideas further. They were nearly all Roman Catholic priests who worked with the poor and oppressed of Latin American countries. They argued that this was not an intellectual theology which was theorized by academics in ivory towers – a charge they make against most European theology – but a practical understanding of Christianity which came from the grass roots.

These priests argued that their Christian principles identified them with those who were struggling for liberation from poverty, oppression and injustice. Involvement in such a struggle made them realize that in this context the challenge to Christianity was not posed by the non-believers but by the 'non-humans' – in other words, the people who had been deprived of their rights as human beings and were not recognized as human by the prevailing social order. They discovered that the Christian message of liberation was meaningless unless it was involved in the transformation of a dehumanizing society. As a result, these priests and theologians were very critical of the Church's involvement in colonial activity and of its apparent support for the regimes which held the people in poverty and oppression. These liberation theologians saw their struggle against injustice mirrored in the biblical accounts of God acting as liberator of Israel in the Exodus and Jesus preaching against the social injustice of his day. They argued that the Bible showed that God has 'a bias towards the poor' and that as Christians they were compelled to identify with the struggle against poverty. They believed that theology was rooted in Christian practice and was following the example of Jesus the Liberator. They argued that the poor could not be free to live as full human beings unless the social and political systems which dehumanized them were transformed. They therefore used many of the ideas of Marxism to offer a criticism of the oppressive regimes which operated in Latin America.

These expressions of liberation theology spread to many parts of the world where Christians were engaged in a struggle against injustice. For instance, Archbishop Desmond Tutu has been a spokesperson for these ideas in his opposition to apartheid in South Africa.

Disagreements among Christians

Critics of this approach accuse liberation theologians of imposing on Christianity political ideas which are not compatible with it. They argue that Christianity is about the spiritual well-being of individuals and that it is not appropriate for Christian leaders to become engaged in political struggle. Many argue that Christianity and politics should be kept separate and that it is wrong to pursue material rather than spiritual goals.

In reply, liberation theologians argue that Christianity is political and always has been. Archbishop Tutu has stated that if anyone can claim that the Bible is not about politics, they must have been reading a different Bible. Liberation theologians also point out that to collude with or even to allow oppressive regimes to exist is also a political act. They condemn the Church's direct or indirect support of a world system which allows so many to suffer in poverty and injustice.

Even more complex is the issue of whether or not Christianity should identify with violent struggle. Some leaders of the Christian liberation movement were and are pacifist. One great symbol of the peaceful struggle against violent oppression was Archbishop Romero, who was gunned down while he was leading a service in his cathedral in 1980. Some Latin American priests have, however, found that their identification with the poor and oppressed of their community has led them to take up arms alongside them. Some have died in armed struggle. To many this is a difficult idea to accept. Many have a profound sense of shock when they see the Latin American art which portrays Christ the Liberator as a freedom-fighter. One such example is given in Alan Brown's book, *The Christian World*. Viewers do not always notice anything unusual about the calm, almost icon-like face of Christ – until they realize that over his shoulder he is carrying a machine gun. Proponents of liberation theology would argue, however, that the more common western symbols of Jesus as King, reigning over creation, and the constant use of political and military imagery in western Christian art are equally violent but in a more 'familiar' form.

All these issues are reflected in the debates about the relationship between the Church and politics which emerge in this country whenever the Church makes a comment about social issues – such as its report *Faith in the City*.

Teaching suggestions

These issues may be too complex to consider in the classroom before sixth form level, but it is important for teachers of Christianity to be aware of them. Many of the old CSE papers on 'Christian Life' tried to present a very simplistic view of Christianity as supporting the 'status quo'.

Key Stage 3

Thomas à Becket, St Francis of Assissi, St Thomas More, William Tyndale, the Methodist and Salvation Army pioneers and present day workers are examples of a form of Christianity which has always struggled to liberate the poor and oppressed.

Key Stage 4

Liberation theology does feature in some current GCSE syllabuses and the SCAA model syllabuses imply that it should be studied when they mention the international dimension of Christianity at Key Stage 4. The issues raised by liberation theology may make an attempt to 'explain' Christianity less comfortable and straightforward, but they also challenge the picture of Christianity as a dull and worn-out tradition.

Women in Christianity

The controversy surrounding the Church of England's decision to ordain women as priests reflects the fact that the questions surrounding the role and authority of women raise very important issues for modern Christianity. The implications of these questions go far beyond the issue of female priesthood, as far as Christianity's understanding of the world, humanity and even God.

The discussions about women in Christianity can be seen as part of a worldwide movement to challenge traditional beliefs about the inferiority of women and thereby improve their quality of life. The years 1975–1985 were designated 'the Decade for Women' by the United Nations.

Ironically, the modern women's movement has its roots in the campaigns of Christian women in the 19th century. Many middle class women were led by their Christian convictions to become involved in missionary work or work for the abolition of slavery or campaign against alcoholism and prostitution. The work of these women led to two important realizations. Firstly, they demonstrated the energy, intelligence and strength which traditional belief claimed they, as women, could not possess, and thereby challenged the argument against their inclusion in higher education or professions such as medicine or law.

Secondly, the women came to realize that they did not possess the rights they were demanding for others.

Out of the Christian philanthropy of these women, there grew a movement for the rights of women themselves. The focus of this movement quickly became the campaign for votes for women. There were some other important outcomes – for instance, a greater involvement by women in the ministry of Protestant churches, especially in America, where the Congregationalist Church was the first to ordain a woman, in 1853. There was also the revival of the role of deaconess in the Church of England in 1862. Most energy and direction, however, went into the fight for female suffrage. When this battle was at last over, even though it did not bring the radical changes in women's lives that were hoped for, the women's movement lost its force and impetus. When it re-emerged in the 1960s it was as an entirely secular movement which tended to reject Christianity completely as one more instrument of women's oppression. By the late 1970s, however, a growing number of Christian women in England, Europe and especially America, were becoming convinced by the feminist perspective of the women's movement, but at the same time maintained that religion was an essential part of the human experience. They demanded their right to remain within the Christian tradition, despite the acceptance of feminist views. These women expressed feelings of pain, anger and betrayal as they realized that the doctrine and practice of their own Christian traditions actually excluded them from full participation in them. They further realized that Christianity had, over the ages, provided a 'divine sanction' for the subjugation and oppression of women. Within this process, it had used biblical material such as 1 Corinthians 11, where it states that 'the head of every man is Christ, but the head of the woman is her husband', and that 'man was not created for woman, but woman for man'. Furthermore, much of the teaching of the Early Church 'fathers', and later medieval theologians, expressed a very negative view of the nature of women. For instance, St Clement of Alexandria taught that 'the female sex is death's deaconess and is especially dishonoured of God'. St Jerome claimed that 'Woman is a temple built over a sewer'. St Augustine maintained that 'the husband should rule over the wife, just as the spirit rules over the flesh' and later St Thomas Aquinas defined woman's nature as 'defective and misbegotten'.

Christian feminists claimed that if Christianity was to become the means of redemption for *all* humanity, which it claimed to be, it must rid itself of sexism. They were therefore arguing that their call for a non-sexist Christianity was a call for *true* Christianity.

This call for a truly inclusive Christianity has implications for every aspect of the religion – for instance, the understanding of the Bible, the language of worship, the ritual and ministry of the Church, the images used to describe God and even the very understanding of the nature of God.

We will look briefly at two examples of these issues: the concept of female discipleship and the imagery used to describe God.

Female discipleship

The question of female discipleship illustrates the call of feminist theology to re-assess the traditional approach to the translation and interpretation of the Bible. It is also very relevant to the debate about female priesthood. Feminist biblical scholars point out that there is strong evidence that Jesus did have female disciples and that, as a result, women had positions of authority in the early Christian community. They argue that this evidence has been ignored or removed by mistranslation. They further claim that this early female leadership was suppressed and eventually removed by the pressure of the sexist culture of the Graeco-Roman world. The 'hidden history' of this process can be found by the 'unwitting testimony' of some of the latest material in the New Testament, the Pastoral Epistles. Here, there are specific rulings against female leadership – e.g. 1 Timothy 2:12, which states: 'I permit no woman to teach or to have authority over men, she is to keep silent.' The feminist scholars argue that such direct prohibitions would not exist unless such a practice was already taking place.

In contrast, they point to the record of Jesus' acceptance of the authority of women, which was remarkable against the background of his contemporaries' beliefs and attitudes. This is reflected in his approach to the woman with a flow of blood (Mark 5:25–34), the Syro-Phoenician woman (Mark 7:24–30), Mary and Martha (Luke 10:38–42) and the Samaritan woman (John 4:4–30), where he defied the traditional attitudes towards women's role and status and spoke to them on the same terms as men. Furthermore, they argue that Mark's Gospel speaks specifically of female disciples (15:40–1). They point out that the words used here to describe the work of the women 'following' and 'ministering' are used elsewhere to describe ideal discipleship. This verse in Mark's Gospel shows that although the male disciples deserted Jesus at his arrest and trial, the women stayed to witness his crucifixion. Finally, all four Gospels agree that women were among the first witnesses of the resurrection. In a culture in which a woman's testimony was not considered to be legally valid, it seems unlikely that such a tradition would be invented – although Paul's account of the resurrection appearances makes no mention of them (1 Corinthians 15:3–9.). The one person mentioned in all four Gospels is Mary Magdalen – and in John's Gospel (John 20:17) she is given a special commission to 'go and tell'. We now know, as a result of archaeological discoveries, that some Christian groups now considered heretical told stories about Mary Magdalen as the Apostle especially commissioned by Jesus. There is also a story about Peter's anger at this and refusal to accept her authority.

Feminist scholars then point to evidence in Paul's letters of women in positions of authority. Despite his arguments elsewhere, there are examples in the greetings at the beginning and end of his letters of female leaders. One of the best examples is in the closing paragraph of the letters to the Romans, in chapter 16. There Paul describes Prisca as a 'co-worker' with himself (verse 4). He also refers to Phoebe (verses 1–2) as a 'deacon' (translated here as a 'servant') and as a 'prostasis', which elsewhere in the New Testament refers to an elder – the forerunner of the bishops – but in this case is translated as 'helper'. In verse 7 he also greets someone as an 'Apostle'; the earliest texts contain the female name Junia, but later translations change this to the male Junias. Thus, the scholars argue, there is evidence both of early female leaders and of the attempts to remove such references.

Imagery used to describe God

Another important area of Christian feminist theology is in the discussion of language and imagery used about God. The feminist theologians argue that the traditional Christian teaching that God is without gender is denied by the almost exclusive use of male language and imagery. This conveys the impression that God is male. Furthermore, the language tends to be not only male but referring to male domination in images such as Father, Lord, King, Prince and Judge. The feminist scholars claim that this gives a distorted image of the nature of God and ignores the diversity of language and imagery used in the Bible to express God's nature. They point to passages such as Isaiah 49:15, which describe God as mother. They also draw attention to biblical references to the female aspect of God in the figure of Wisdom (e.g. in the Book of Wisdom in the Apocrypha, chapters 8 and 9). They also remind us of the use by mystics such as Julian of Norwich and by

St Anselm of the title Mother to address Jesus or God. They argue that it is important to incorporate female language and imagery in Christian worship in order to make the religion truly inclusive and to prevent a distorted understanding of the nature of God.

Christian feminist theology is now recognized as an important branch of scholarship in many universities in America and a growing number in Great Britain. Its actual teaching may be known by only a minority at present, but the implications of its challenge to Christian beliefs and practices are very important and far-reaching – as is illustrated by the debate about women priests.

We would argue that teachers of Christianity need to be aware of these important challenges and questions. Many of the more recent educational books on Christianity try to present more positive images of women in their language and illustration. There is, however, a dilemma involved in an attempt to present good Religious Education and in maintaining non-sexist education. On the one hand, pupils should be presented with positive images of women; on the other, they need to appreciate that Christianity is still dominated by men because the teachings and practices of the Church have made it very difficult for women to have equal opportunities. Pupils should at least be aware of a significant movement within Christianity which challenges the traditional attitudes to the role and authority of women.

Teaching suggestions

It is not the role of the RE teacher to take sides in the women in Christianity debate, or the other subjects dealt with in this chapter, though syllabuses are never neutral, as the nationalistic nature of the National Curriculum clearly demonstrates.

Key Stage 1

Consideration should be given to children meeting women as well as men in leadership positions, either when they visit places of worship or when Christians are invited into the school. This should, of course, inform decisions at all key stages.

Teachers can also use story to help provide children with positive images of women. Some of the stories mentioned on pages 40 and 41 are appropriate here, for example *Mama Do You Love Me?* by Barbara Joose (Little, Brown and Company, 1992), *Amazing Grace* by Mary Hoffman (Frances Lincoln, 1991) and *The Whales' Song* by Dyan Sheldon and Gary Blythe (Hutchinson, 1990).

Key Stage 2

It is not possible – or appropriate – to attempt to disguise the fact that the Bible and Christian history have been written almost exclusively by and for men, and from a male perspective. Nor is it appropriate to address this issue at Key Stage 2.

If teachers are aware of this issue, however, they can be careful to avoid exclusive language themselves. For example, they can avoid using a personal pronoun when referring to God, or using terms such as 'brotherhood' and 'mankind'. Teachers may find the books mentioned in the bibliography on page 149 helpful in uncovering the 'hidden history' of women in Christianity – especially Barbara MacHaffie's book *Herstory: Women in the Christian Tradition* (Fortress, 1986).

Key Stage 3

As pupils move through Key Stage3, teachers can deal more explicitly with the 'hidden' stories of women in the Christian tradition. For example, the female disciples mentioned in Mark chapter 15, verse 40 and the female leaders referred to in Paul's letter to the Romans, chapter 16.

Key Stage 4

At Key Stage 4 pupils can begin to consider the arguments involved in women's position in Christianity. The biblical arguments for male authority need to be explored in a fair and balanced way. On the other hand, theargument that this biblical material can be interpreted in different ways can also be addressed. For example, pupils can consider the different accounts of the creation of mankind in Genesis chapters 1 and 2 (see pages 60–4). Again, teachers may find the books mentioned on page 149 helpful in addressing these issues.

Further reading

For the teacher

General
The Quiet Revolution, R Banks, Lion, 1985 and 1989.

Inter-religious encounter
All their Splendours, David Brown, Fount, 1982.
The Bible and People of Other Faiths, W Ariarajah, World Council of Churches, 1985.

What is Idolatry?, Roger Hooker, The British Council of Churches, 1986. Hooker was a CMS missionary for many years, during which time he also studied Hinduism and Sanskrit. The book is available from the bookshop at Inter-Church House, 35–41 Lower Marsh, London SE1 7RL.

Liberation theology

The Christian World, Alan Brown, MacDonald, 1984.

Images of Jesus, A Wessels, SCM Press, 1990.

Introducing Liberation Theology, C and L Boff, Burns and Oates, 1987.

Theology and Politics, D B Forester, Blackwell, 1988.

Voices from the Margin – Interpreting the Bible in the Third World, ed. R S Sugirtharajah, SPCK, 1991.

Women in Christianity

Feminist Interpretation of the Bible, ed. L Russell, Blackwell, 1986.

Feminist Theology, A Reader, ed. A Loades, SPCK, 1990.

Herstory: Women in the Christian Tradition, B MacHaffie, Fortress, 1986.

The Divine Feminine: The Biblical Imagery of God as Female, V R Mollencott, Crossroads, 1983.

Womanspirit Rising – A Feminist Reader in Religion, C Christ and J Plaskow, Harper, 1979.

Women and Spirituality, U King, Macmillan, 1989.

For the classroom

Being a Christian, A Wood, BFSS National RE Centre (address in Appendix 2), 1990. The personal beliefs of a number of Christians from different backgrounds (Key Stage 3/4).

Christianity, a Living Faith, B Wintersgill, Macmillan, 1989 (Key Stage 4). Presents Christianity as a broad and diverse religion.

15 Christianity in a world religions context: mission and dialogue

Introduction

Religions do not leave the cultures with which they come in contact unchanged. They, in turn, are influenced by the cultures which they encounter. An obvious example of these statements is the developments in Religious Education in Britain since about 1970. One of these has been the inclusion of other religions than Christianity in syllabuses, now a legal requirement. The other, almost universally welcomed, has been the change from teaching the Bible and some Christian history to introducing children to Christianity as a world religion and studying all of its dimensions. We would argue that this would not yet have happened had it not been for the world religions approach taken to the other principal religions found in Britain today.

Christianity was originally an entirely Jewish movement. Within a century of the crucifixion, however, most Christians were probably Gentiles who had no Jewish blood in their bodies and were probably proud of it. Christianity now began to adopt a Romano-Greek cultural identity. Its concept of priesthood, even to the vestments which priests wear to this day, is derived very largely from this non-Jewish milieu. Greek had been the language of the Jewish dispersion scattered across the Roman Empire and beyond it. Many of the Jews who were preached to by St Paul may have been happier using the Greek version of their scriptures, known as the Septuagint, rather than the mainly Hebrew original. However, by about 405CE the Latin Vulgate of St Jerome was set to dominate the Christian west until the Reformation of the 15th century. One characteristic of the Reformation was the translation of the Bible into the national languages of the people. Martin Luther began the movement with his German Bible. In England he was followed by William Tyndale, who paid with his life, though others earlier had produced English translations. The development of the English language owes much to the Authorized (or King James) version of the Bible, published in 1611.

When European missionaries went to India or Africa, one of the first things they did was write down languages which hitherto had often been used only orally. This they did in order to make the Bible available to the people among whom they were working, and because their concept of civilization was based upon literacy.

Next, the missionaries set up schools at the same time that others of their number were translating the Bible, or at least the New Testament. Often, however, the use of regional languages was the only cultural concession which Protestant Christians made. The churches which they established were European in architecture and liturgy. In 1972 it was possible to attend a eucharist in English at Lahore cathedral or Delhi cathedral at which the liturgy was the Book of Common Prayer of 1662 and the celebrant was white, even though most of the congregation was Pakistani or Indian. Now the situation has changed to the extent that the clergy are of the same race as the congregation, though the vestments and use of English at some services still reflect the British origins of their Christianity. However, in 1972 it was also possible to visit a village not very far from Lahore and be shown a church which was 'L'-shaped, with men sitting on the earth floor in one leg of the letter, women in the other (unable to see one another) and the communion table at the point where the two legs joined. The service was in Urdu, the hymns and the tunes were composed by Pakistani Christians and belonged to their own culture, not to *Hymns Ancient and Modern*. Many similar experiences can be enjoyed in India, Africa and other parts of the world today, and in some British cities. This has sometimes been described as shaking off the Constantinian or Latin or generally European captivity. Changing European vestments for ochre robes may raise some eyebrows and certainly the suggestion that the Vedas should replace the Old Testament received short shrift among (white) church leaders! The argument was that it was through the Hindu scriptures that they had come to know God, not through those of Judaism.

It is now possible to find Indian music and musical instruments being used in Christian worship, with congregations seated on the ground singing bhajans (devotional songs). Indian dance forms and traditional Indian art are also used to present Christian themes, stories from the Bible and incidents in the life of Jesus. The effect is wholesome in the view of many people, who begin to feel that Christianity is actually a religion of India, not something alien and out of place. The same kind of experiences are part of the Christian story in Africa and South America. Among Roman Catholics assimilation of local cultures, as happened in Britain 1,400 years ago, has often been more usual that it has among Protestants, who tended to impose the ways and customs of their own countries, as some American evangelical missionaries may still be doing, believing them to be biblical.

There is no need to go to India to discover that Christianity is culturally diverse. Visit France or Germany, especially at Christmas or Easter, and you will find the same Christian message dressed in different cultural clothes.

Why should teachers be concerned about presenting Christianity as a world religion? The answer should be obvious in London, Leicester or Bradford and other cities where there are black Christians. Many of those from the Caribbean can tell stories of being discouraged from attending churches when they arrived in Britain because they might scare white people away. These are true stories. More recently, a student showed a CAFOD Christmas card of a black Mary and baby Jesus to a 10-year-old child who refused to accept that Jesus might have been black. They were 'Pakis' and he was fed up with Pakis getting into everything! Another boy said that it couldn't be Jesus, he was the wrong colour. There is little chance of presenting a Christianity which respects all people if Jesus is always white. 'There is no such thing as Jew or Greek, slave and freeman, male and female; for you are all one person in Christ Jesus' (Galatians 3:28) is the message of St Paul.

Teachers are often distressed about the racism and the narrow nationalism which they encounter in children. We might ask whether we teach Christianity in a way which endorses and even fosters such attitudes? Christianity was not first preached by a white European and the majority of Christians in the world today are not white.

Teaching suggestions

Children should not be allowed to equate Christianity with white western culture from the outset. To undo or un-teach something is difficult, once the mind becomes set.

Key Stage 1

Colour photographs of Christians at worship in many parts of the world can now be self-made from photographs in books, thanks to the relative cheapness of making colour enlargements today. Christmas cards can be enlarged in the same way and displayed round the classroom. At the time of visiting a church it would be easy to say 'If we went to Africa...' (or wherever our photographs come from), 'this would be what the church might look like; this is the priest we might meet', or 'This is the picture of Jesus we might find in the church'. Our clergy visitor might be black, but would probably be UK-born, though some overseas Christians come to Britain on exchange visits and it might be possible to contact one of them through a local church.

Beware of projecting the 'Third World image' of poverty and backwardness upon which racism thrives. Africa and India are recovering from the exploitation which often accompanied the benefits which some people concede that colonial rule and European missions brought.

Key Stage 2

The same policy can be adopted but added to by the use of videos of Christianity in other parts of the world and stories of Christians from some of these countries. Festivals as practised in them are sometimes to be found in travel or geographical magazines (e.g. *National Geographic*, December 1983, 'Easter in a Greek Village'). The *Believe it or Not* series produced by ITV has looked at aspects of non-British Christianity. Someone who has been to France or Spain, for example, might be able to share their experiences. For many Britons, multiculturalism begins at Calais.

Britain itself was once the focus of mission, of course. There were three phases: one of unknown origin in the Roman period was the first. It survives in the story of St Alban, St Patrick, and the house church at Lullingstone villa in Kent. The second was the conversion of the Irish by St Patrick and the subsequent mission to Scotland and Northumbria. The third was the Roman mission of St Augustine to Canterbury. Stories connected with these could result in lively RE if imaginatively used.

Key Stage 3

We might use the same kind of material more analytically. Many customs such as well-dressing in Derbyshire and the Grasmere rush-bearing ceremony and most of the traditions of Christmas are pre-Christian. How they originated, what they signified, why they have persisted but been reinterpreted could be interesting topics for study, especially in areas where these survivals are to be found.

Key Stage 4

The motives of missionaries now and in Victorian times, the concern of people in Roman, Saxon or Viking Britain when faced with a new religion, and the responses of contemporary inhabitants of South America or India to family members converting to the new faith could be explored. It must be challenging and will often be painful. This is a time when mission could be studied and the impact upon the cultures which missionaries encountered, including the effect of missionaries to Britain. Many ministers in British churches are former missionaries. They may be prepared to come to school to describe their training and their work and to discuss the sense of vocation which led to them going abroad.

Issues

Two inter-related matters are the work of Christian missionaries and the activities of Christian aid organizations. Missionaries have often been maligned. It is possible to come across blacks and Asians who have not converted but who are appreciative of the renaissance which took place in their own religious tradition in response to the Christian presence. There are others who were educated by the missionaries and were not conscious of pressure being put upon them to become Christians. It is, of course, necessary to acknowledge that mistakes were made, but missionaries were men and women of their time; few Britons in those days doubted the right to establish an empire and colonize as much of the world as possible, if only to stop supposedly less civilized foreigners doing it! The missionaries were seen to be bearers of civilization, something which was defined in the terms of the white man. However, times have changed. The stories of Livingstone or Albert Schweitzer which were used 30 years ago might now be considered racist. There is a place for looking at the idea of mission and using Mother Theresa as an example of Christian commitment and love, but not, we would suggest, in a topic on India or Hinduism, and never with the implication that only Christians care. During the recent Bosnian crisis Muslim and inter-religious groups in Britain have been giving help to the Bosnian Muslims. In Israel and the Occupied Territories there are Jews, Christians and Muslims co-operating to create a just and peaceful society. The work of the Red Crescent seldom captures the news headlines; it is the work of the Red Cross which is newsworthy in Britain. If the school has Muslim pupils they may be able to present a more realistic and balanced picture than that of which teachers are aware.

Care must also be taken to avoid giving the impression that the colonialized blacks were feckless and lazy, one of the justifications given for empire. Using photographs of them living in shanty accommodation today can reinforce the image. Christian Aid Week is a time for being especially sensitive.

It is not easy for teachers to redress the balance. There are few stories about 20th-century Muslims, Jews, Hindus, Buddhists or Sikhs who have cared for the needy. Why is this? Partly it is media interest; the Sikhs or Hindus of Calcutta who care for the homeless are not news. The Albanian nun is. Partly it has to do with wealth. If some Hindus share their piece of bread with another Hindu both will starve. Of course, there are rich Hindus who seem indifferent to the suffering on their doorsteps, but there are rich Christians in Britain who are also apparently careless about their fellow citizens who are homeless, and whose cardboard homes they pass by daily.

16 The sixth form

Religious Education was always intended to form part of a young person's education until leaving school. The 1988 Act made this clear and Circular 1/94 endorses the view. Its provisions apply to all 'registered pupils in maintained schools' under the age of 19 (paragraphs 5 and 11, pages 9 and 10). Religious Education must, therefore, be included in the sixth form curriculum. The challenge is for teachers to make it interesting for young people who are likely to claim that they have enough to cope with in studying for A levels and cannot see the point of doing other things. Part of the answer to this comment lies in the general approach of the school, governors and parents. If everything is examination and market-place orientated from Year 7, then it is not surprising that a 'liberal education' is despised. Even where the law is obeyed, however, Religious Education must be strong enough to hold its own on educational not legal grounds.

The roots of success lie in the first year of the secondary school. If the new intake is provided with a prospectus for Religious Education which lays down its purpose and the ground rules, and the first term is one which concentrates on the methodology of studying religion – based on the skills, attitudes,and concepts on page 57, related, perhaps, to a case study of religion locally or in Britain – then there is hope that the future of the subject will be secure. Of course, the assurance of an open approach has to be followed by good practice, so it may not be convincing to concentrate on Christianity in year one, term one. Some teachers justify this on the grounds that this is likely to be the religion, if any, that the intake will know about. This may possibly be true, though our own experiences cause us to have our doubts. But we would want to use some painless and enjoyable method of testing to discover whether any assumptions we had were correct. Photographs linked with churches and other aspects of religion in the locality and famous figures like the Pope, the Dalai Lama and the Virgin Mary might be used for identification. We would also be conscious of the luggage-carrying and distancing issues that we mentioned in Chapters 1 and 2. Those, if they exist, are unlikely to be removed by a study of the life of Jesus, however investigative and exciting. An examination of the multi-religious nature of the locality would seem a good way to convince pupils of openness. A 'map' of the world's major religions, followed by their distribution and arrival in Britain and then their place in the locality, might provide the second stage of our Religious Studies course. Christianity would feature importantly throughout, of course.

The next challenge is that of selecting GCSE subjects. We can only hope for three things here. The first is that Religious Studies enjoys such esteem among pupils and our colleagues that there is a demand for it which management is willing to support. The second is that it will be set against subjects in such a way that it has a fair chance of being chosen. The third is that the GCSE course enables us to remain true to the principles of our prospectus (this is often a time when teachers revert to a study of the Gospels) and that non-examination Religious Studies can remain worthwhile. Pupils who did not take the subject at GCSE level may even opt to study it for A level. This seems to happen quite frequently in our experience and, of course, the future of Religious Education depends upon students coming forward to take Religious Studies as at least part of a degree, or as primary school teachers, remembering the subject with enjoyment and so becoming teachers and wanting to introduce their children to it.

We would suggest that in all these matters an eye is kept on History and Geography and the provision they receive for teaching the subject. Religious Studies should have the same quality of staffing, time and resources. With these things in place, the sixth form lesson should be one which students can anticipate as worthwhile.

There may be items for specifically Christian discussion, such as those mentioned in Chapter 14 – for example, liberation theology, attitudes to other religions and the role of women in Christianity. Other areas touched on in other chapters might be added: mission, Christian diversity, the future of Christianity. However, there is a danger that some of these can be remote and unimportant if students are not Christians. To many outsiders the Anglican ordination of women dispute has been an embarrassment. They feel that they are being required to witness what is actually a private grief or joy. If, after a few opening lessons at the beginning of the year, the class can be persuaded to write its own agenda, that might be better than imposing a course. We would suggest that hesitation might be met with a list of items from which students might anonymously state their preferences in writing. The list might include an open discussion on the relevance of Christianity to contemporary life.

Topics which span religions and go beyond them may be more popular than those which confine themselves to one religion or even several, as well as the introduction of a previously unstudied religion such as Jainism or the Baha'i faith. New Religious Movements should find a place somewhere in the Religious Studies syllabus, partly because they tend to attract young people but also because education is the best antidote to brainwashing, whether it be by the tabloid press or by NRMs which allegedly use the technique. Totalitarian governments control education so strictly because they wish to impose their beliefs on young people. If the study of religion is concerned with accuracy we should be anxious to enable pupils to understand why new movements appear and what some of them teach. NRMs are often eager to provide literature and speakers. Teachers may wish to take advantage of such offers, but the headteacher and parents should be consulted and all concerned should know how to conduct themselves. The teacher should be well enough briefed to be able to intervene if any danger of 'brainwashing' is perceived.

Some teachers claim to wish to enable pupils to make informed choices about beliefs and values. If they do have this aim, they should be introducing sixth formers at least to non-religious life stances and interpretations of the world. In those large areas of Britain which are multifaith it should be possible to arrange for speakers from more than the six principal traditions to visit the school to speak about how they make sense of life. Even in places which are deprived of such rich resources, it should not be difficult to find a Buddhist, a Humanist and a Baha'i, as well as a Christian, to contribute. Some national agencies which can help are listed at the end of this book; others can be found in *Teaching World Religions*, ed. Clive Erricker, Heinemann Educational, 1993. Even if our aim is not to help young people make choices about life our course should, as a by-product, provide them with the skills to do so. The personal experiences and views of believer visitors should help all pupils to put the religions which they have studied into world-outlook perspectives. Returning to Christianity, we would strongly affirm that no young person should leave our schools unaware of what it means to be a Christian in terms of beliefs and values, and ignorant of the practices of the religion. But neither should they be ignorant of other religions and non-religious life-stances, and they should possess the skills which are required to study others if we have been successful in communicating an enthusiasm to do so.

Finally, we would offer some specifically Christian subjects for consideration:

- Christian responses to ethical matters, especially those at the frontiers of knowledge such as genetic engineering
- the problem of evil and suffering
- science and religion
- the purpose of life.

Further reading

For the teacher

Teaching World Religions, ed. Clive Erricker, Heinemann Educational, 1993.

For the classroom

Christianity and Homosexuality, Lesbian and Gay Christian Movement, Oxford House, Derbyshire Street, London E2 6HG, 1992. A resource for students which may be used from Key Stage 4 and perhaps in a course of ethics, but more likely in sixth form studies.

Video

Humanism, the Great Detective Story, The British Humanist Association, Lamb's Conduit Passage, London WC1R 4RH. 21 minutes (also at Key Stage 4).

Conclusion

Those readers who have worked their way through the whole of this book may be asking at least two questions.

First: isn't the approach confessional?

We would deny this charge. As we understand it, the term 'confessional' refers to a presentation of the Christian religion (or any other faith) in such a way that its truth is not open to question. Confessional is 'used to connote instruction in particular beliefs to the exclusion of all others', to quote the late Robin Shepherd writing in *The Dictionary of Religious Education*, page 94, ed. John Sutcliffe, SCM Press, 1984. In this book our brief has been to help teachers to present Christianity as a world religion. Were they to teach it as the only religion, they would be confessional in their approach, but they would also be behaving illegally, as a number of quotations from government documents provided in Part 1 of this book clearly state. If we are accused by some Christians of drawing too much attention to the warts on the face of their religion we might take heart that we have perhaps got right the balance between idealizing it and being realistic. We believe that an objective study (whatever that may mean) would have resulted in courses which were anodyne and anaemic and utterly unrepresentative of Christianity as a living faith, which has never been free from controversy.

Secondly, we would hope that teachers are not assuming any kind of religious or other belief on the part of the children they teach. Furthermore, they should be respectful of the views and beliefs which all pupils bring with them to school. No one should be marginalized or harrassed because of their particular faith or lack of it.

The second question is apparently more practical. How can teachers cover everything even in eleven years and without five other religions to study? This is, of course, a problem that will face anyone who uses the kind of Agreed Syllabuses which the government wants to encourage, to judge from the SCAA model syllabuses.

The solution which we offer, which should be a practical possibility at Key Stages 3 and 4 and even, perhaps, at Key Stage 2, is this:

Take a topic – for example, 'Worship' – and through it try to present the essence of Christianity.

- The church is a building where Christians meet.
- They meet because of certain beliefs about Jesus.
- They come with certain ideas about God which they derive from the stories Jesus told about God and the things which he did (forgiving people, loving them, making them whole).
- They read about these teachings in the Bible.
- There are some special occasions on which they gather in addition to Sunday – the festivals of Easter and Christmas.
- They hold special services – baptism and the Lord's Supper – besides others, when they hear sermons and sing hymns.
- These services and their faith in Jesus sustain them so that they can live their daily lives and love other people as Jesus taught them to.

We would argue that through these seven points we have covered the main features of Christianity and can use them to convey the Christian world view. Even at Key Stage 1, there are many aspects that could be examined in such a way that the topic becomes much more than a naming of parts.

What we have done through worship could as easily be conveyed through a topic on Jesus, the Bible, Easter, Christmas or Christian ethics, to name but a few. Teachers need not, therefore, be overwhelmed by the sheer bulk of religious content which appears in syllabuses or in this book.

Finally, our words should be read in the context of government policy and our own belief that the purpose of Religious Education should be to help pupils study beliefs and values, many of which will be religious, but not all. We hope that what we have written of Christianity could hold true of any other belief and values system.

Appendix 1: Jehovah's Witnesses and Religious Education

There are two reasons for including this section in our book. Firstly, teachers and students often tell us that having Jehovah's Witnesses in the class causes problems. Secondly, we know from our own observations that Jehovah's Witnesses are sometimes treated with intolerance. Two led a seminar at a conference on women in religion. Those who were responsible for seminars on feminist theology, women in Buddhism and women in Islam enjoyed sessions in which the Religious Studies rules were followed. The Jehovah's Witnesses found themselves under an attack which sometimes became personal. Families can tell of experiences where children have been victimized.

It is not always acknowledged that many Witnesses were imprisoned in Nazi concentration camps. Unlike the Jews, they sometimes had an opportunity to gain freedom, simply by denying their faith. Jehovah's Witnesses are also instructed to be respectful of authority and may accept it even when it is unjust (Romans 13:1–6).

It is difficult to discover why Witnesses are treated differently from Muslims or Jews, for example, but they often are. One reason may be a basic prejudice on the part of teachers of a liberal outlook. Another may simply be that these children are one stress too many in a demanding classroom life. We leave it to you to consider the reasons, if you wish, while we proceed to explain the situation and suggest how schools can respond.

Beliefs

It is important that the following beliefs are understood, because the conduct of a Jehovah's Witness, like that of any person, is based upon belief and world view and can only be understood when these are appreciated.

- Jesus is God's son, who died for the sins of humanity and provides an example of a life dedicated to the service of his father, Jehovah.
- The Bible is completely accurate and should guide the Christian's daily life. It is also a prophetic book and Witnesses take very seriously the passages which refer to the coming of the Kingdom of God and the creation of a new heaven and a new earth (e.g. Revelation 21 and 22).

• The Bible requires Christians to live in the world and contribute to its well-being but not to be part of it, as Jesus taught (John 15:19, 17:16). The whole world lies in the power of the wicked one (John 12:31, 1 John 5:19, 2 Corinthians 4:4).

Morality and conduct

Again we confine ourselves to matters which are likely to affect the school.

Morality is uncompromisingly biblical. Therefore, such things as homosexuality, adultery, extramarital sex and drug-taking are rejected. This has consequences for PSE and sex education. They should be taught with attention being given to biblical teachings and not in a moral vacuum.

The authority of civil powers is respected and this, of course, includes the school. Children are seldom, if ever, disruptive or rude.

Because Jehovah's Witnesses serve the Kingdom of God, they do not join a country's armed forces and are neutral in any observance of nationalism. This would be extended to singing the school song. Christmas and Easter are not celebrated, though Witnesses are thankful to God for the birth, death and resurrection of Jesus. They point to the fact that celebrations are accompanied by pagan rites, that the first evidence for the celebration of Christmas dates from 336CE and is certainly not biblical. If one were to find a Jehovah's Witness service taking place on Christmas or Easter Day it would be a coincidence. The days would have fallen on one of those when normal worship and Bible study was being held.

The only mention of birthdays in the Bible are those of Pharaoh (Genesis 14:18–22) and Herod Antipas (Mark 6:21–8, the well-known Salome story). Both are examples of the individual being given excessive importance. This is not to be encouraged, so birthdays are not observed in any way, not even by offering the greeting 'Happy birthday'.

Jehovah's Witnesses take the command to be separate to the point of not joining in worship with other Christians, just as many Christians will not take part in inter-faith acts of worship. For Jehovah's Witnesses, school worship is therefore something in which they cannot share. Children do not participate in competitions and extra-curricular sports, for the same reasons. This includes raffles, though children will willingly give to good causes.

One of the best-known aspects of Jehovah Witness practice is the refusal to accept blood transfusions. This follows the Jewish practice of abstaining from blood and the injunction of Acts 15:19, 20, 28, 29.

Solutions

First of all, teachers who say 'What a pity it is about these children, they miss so much' might realize that they have their own culture, just as other people do. Children are brought up in it and have the support of their families and the wider community. By the time they come to school they are likely to have been prepared already and to be aware of the positive aspects of their lifestyle, not the negative one which outsiders notice.

Secondly, it might be sensitive to excuse children from school when the carol service is being held, just as children of other religions might be allowed to stay away from it (if this is legally possible). If it was an event which was held outside school hours into which children and teachers opted voluntarily, much embarrassment could be avoided.

School worship is an activity from which Jehovah's Witness children must be withdrawn. They are not alone in this respect. We ask teachers to consider how sensitive they are to children who are withdrawn. We have known situations where they are required to stand outside the hall throughout the service and then called in for the notices, to be stared at by their classmates. Do they need to come into the hall at all? Is it necessary to address the whole school on any secular matter, and do the children listen if we do? Because it is traditional, is it necessarily the best way of giving out notices? If teachers want the whole school or year group to gather, must it be for an act of worship? There are ways of expressing the corporate unity of the school without drawing attention to particular groups, who are made to seem to deny it. If school worship must continue at all, its presentation as an activity which children could opt into rather than out of might enhance the value of worship, and some of the practical difficulties which attach to it might disappear.

We would ask class teachers whether they positively explain, at the child's ability level, why some children differ in their lifestyles to others. It might help prevent bullying and promote respect. (We are aware of vegetarians, as well as members of religious groups, who are allowed to seem odd by teachers with certain views of what normality is.) In a pluralist society 'normal' is becoming an increasingly difficult term to use.

Religious Education

Many parents, some Jehovah's Witnesses among them, still believe that the purpose of RE is religious nurture or instruction. They naturally withdraw their children. If the school policy statement which all parents should receive and, in secondary schools, the Religious Studies department's outline of purpose and content (just one side of A4), show that RE is about understanding religions, as laid down by law, then many Witness children may participate. We have known some who have taken it at O level and GCSE and an excellent Religious Studies student who was a Jehovah's Witness remains in the mind. Of course there are activities such as making Christmas or Easter cards which children should not be asked to do, but teachers can easily find other things which are acceptable.

The golden rule is to talk with parents and then, if necessary, with the local elders. Tell them what you teach in RE and what its purpose is and seek their co-operation. Within the limits mentioned in this section it should be possible to come to positive solutions, and once this agreement has been reached it is likely to be communicated from one generation of parents to another. At the end of the day, of course, parents have the right to withdraw their children and this must always be respected positively.

At Key Stage 4, if not Key Stage 3, there is a place for doing a study of Jehovah's Witnesses as part of the RE course, whether there are the children of Witnessses in the school or not, and inviting in a member of the denomination to participate who, like the class, knows what the purpose is and how to approach the lesson in a proper religious studies manner.

Seventh Day Adventists and Plymouth Brethren

These are smaller in numbers nationally but often strong locally. Usually they do not wish their children to take part in RE or collective worship. Some would wish to have separate schools. We would encourage the teacher to meet parents and community leaders to discuss what can be done. If the solution has to be withdrawal, we hope that this can be done as positively as possible by parents and the school. Once again, these denominations provide opportunities for study at Key Stage 4.

Further reading

School and Jehovah's Witnesses (which really addresses the USA situation but lays down the basic principles) and *Jehovah's Witnesses Unitedly Doing God's Will Worldwide*, which is a brief introduction to their beliefs and practices. *Jehovah's Witnesses, Proclaimers of God's Kingdom* is a 750-page survey published in 1993. These can be obtained free of charge from members of the local community or from The Watch Tower Society, The Ridgeway, London NW7 1RN.

We would like to express our gratitude to Witnesses in Chichester for their friendly help.

Appendix 2: Useful addresses and courses

Addresses

Articles of Faith: Bury Business Centre, Kay Street, Bury BL9 6BU (tel: 061 705 1878; fax 061 763 3421). Artefacts, posters, videos, in fact almost every resource the teacher of Religious Education requires. Send for catalogue. Also provides helpful advice.

British and Foreign Schools Society National RE Centre (also *West London RE Centre*): West London Institute of High Education, Lancaster House, Borough Road, Isleworth, Middlesex TW7 5DU.

Christian Education Movement: Royal Buildings, Derby DE1 1GW. The leading RE support agency for teachers. We would encourage schools to subscribe to its mailings.

Jewish Education Bureau: 8 Westcombe Avenue, Leeds LS8 2BS. A full catalogue is available on request. Can also provide details of the Anne Frank travelling exhibition.

The National Society's RE Centre: 30 Causton Street, London SW1P 4AU.

The Regional RE Centre: Westhill College, Weoley Park Road, Selly Oak, Birmingham B29 6LL.

The Welsh National Centre for RE: School of Education, University College of North Wales, Deiniol Road, Bangor, Gwynedd LL57 2UW.

See also *Teaching World Religions*, ed. Clive Erricker, Heinemann Educational, 1993 for addresses of religious organizations.

Courses on Christianity for teachers

Teachers seeking a qualification in Religious Studies might consider contacting either of the following for details of their distance learning courses:

The Association of Christian Teachers: Wesley Place, Stapleford, Nottingham NG9 8DP. Offers a Diploma in Religious Education course which includes units on Religious Education, Christianity and other world religions. The course director is Dr Trevor Cooling, to whom enquiries should be addressed.

The School of Theology, Westminster College, Oxford OX2 9AT. Provides a course in Christian Studies. Details can be obtained from the secretary.

Bibliography

Part 1

For the teacher

A Dictionary of Religious Education, ed. John Sutcliffe, SCM Press, 1984.

Discernment volume 6, number 1, 1992, 'Focus on Religious Education'. This Christian Journal of Inter-Religious Encounter is published by the Committee for Relations of People of Other Faiths of the Council of Churches for Britain and Ireland, in conjunction with Westminster College, North Hinksey, Oxford. Further details can be obtained from the editor, Dr Clinton Bennett, at that address. The list on page 18 of Chapter 2 appeared in the edition of *Discernment* cited above.

Reforming Religious Education, Edwin Cox and Josephine Cairns, Kogan Page 1989, places the present position of Religious Education in its historical context.

Religious Education in Secondary Schools, Schools Council Working Paper 36, Evans/Methuen, 1971, is a seminal document for Religious Education.

Teaching World Religions, ed. Clive Erricker, Heinemann Educational, 1993, has been used extensively in preparing the bibliographies in this book. Section one contains several essays which should be helpful to teachers in working out their personal classroom philosophies. A book which should be at hand in all schools.

Video

Multi-Faith RE, good news for the Christian teacher, St Peter's Saltley Trust. Five Christian teachers talk about their experience of teaching RE in primary schools. Valuable for helping teachers to work out their own attitudes to teaching Religious Education.

Part 2

Chapters 3 and 4 (with sections relating to other chapters)

For the teacher

Christianity, P Moore, Ward Lock, 1982. The stress is on Christian art and architecture and the liturgies related to them, but it is also a very interesting introduction to the religion itself.

The Christians, P McKenzie, SPCK, 1988. A study of phenomena and concepts.

The Quiet Revolution, R Banks, Lion, 1985 and 1989. A survey of Christianity as a world faith addressing itself to global issues and black and orthodox churches. The perspective is evangelical. Since the book was written there have been considerable changes in eastern Europe. (Useful material for several chapters, esp. 12, 13, 14, and 15.)

World Christian Encyclopaedia, ed. D B Barrett, OUP, 1982. A costly, comprehensive compendium.

Approaches to teaching Christianity

A few publications of a general nature which teachers should find of practical help in planning lessons are:

Exploring Christianity, CEM, Exploring a Theme. A primary school mailing is particularly valuable in the context of this book.

Good Practice in Primary Religious Education, 4–11, ed. D Bastide, Falmer Press, 1992.

Religious Education and the Pupil with Learning Difficulties, A S Brown, OUP, 1987.

Religious Education in the Primary Curriculum, W Owen Cole and Judith Evans Lowndes, RMEP/Chansitor, second edition, 1994.

Religious Education Topics for the Primary school and *Religious Education across the Curriculum*, J Rankin, A Brown and M Hayward, Longman, 1989 and 1991.

RE Today, Christian Education Movement and *Exploring a Theme*, which is deliberately aimed at primary schools. (See list of addresses in Appendix 2.)

Teaching Christianity, ed. C Erricker, Lutterworth, 1987.

Gift to the Child: Religious Education in the Primary School, M Grimmitt, J Grove, J Hull and L Spencer, Simon and Schuster (teachers' source book), 1991. The teachers' book which accompanies a large recommended project pack of materials.

The Junior RE Handbook, ed. R Jackson and D Starkings, Stanley Thornes, 1990.

For the classroom

All these cover aspects of Christianity but naturally, other religions are often included too.

Christianity, A Brown and J Perkins, Batsford, 1988. A valuable dictionary (Key Stage 3/4).

Christianity, W Owen Cole, Stanley Thornes, 1989. A presentation of Christianity as a world religion covering contemporary issues such as race and gender (Key Stage 4/GCSE).

Christianity, R O Hughes, Longman, 1991. Very accessible to pupils at Key Stage 4 and especially GCSE.

Christianity, J Jenkins, Heinemann, 1989. Makes considerable use of source material (Key Stage 4).

Christianity, a Pictorial Guide, CEM. A pictorial resource book (Key Stage 2 and upwards).

Christianity in Today's World, S Jenkins and L Smith, BBC Educational Publishing, 1992. Book plus a five-part video of Christianity in a number of countries – England, Brazil, S Africa, southern USA (Key Stage 4 onwards).

Christians, J Drane, Lion, 1994. A broad view but as it at least borders on the confessional it is probably more suitable for denominational schools than others (Key Stage 2/3).

Christians in Britain Today, ed. D Cush, Hodder and Stoughton, 1991. An approach through interviews with Christians (Key Stage 3/4).

Collins Bible Handbook, J Musset, Collins, 1988.

Dimensions of Christianity, Sister Anne Burke and Kevin Mayhew, 1988. Written for Roman Catholic students taking GCSE. Useful for a study of Roman Catholic Christianity at Key Stage 4 or GCSE and for teachers who know little about the largest Christian denomination in the world.

Exploring Religions, O Bennett, Bell and Hyman, 1984. A series of five books plus a teachers' guide (Key Stage 2/3).

Growing up in Christianity, J Holm and R Ridley, Longman, 1990. Brings out the cultural diversity of Christianity through using first-hand experiences (Key Stage 2/3).

Instant Art: Teaching Christianity, Helen Thacker, Palm Tree Press, 1991. Illustrations which can be photocopied and used by children. Helpful explanatory notes (Key Stage 2/3).

Skills in Religious Studies, Books One, Two and Three, J Fageant and C Mercier, Heinemann Educational, 1988 to 1990 (Key Stage 3).

The Christian World, A Brown, Macdonald, 1984. An excellent information book which presents Christianity as a world-wide religion (Key Stage 2/3).

The Christians, P Mckenzie, SPCK, 1988. Relates the diversity of practices and beliefs to phenomena and concepts.

Video

Christianity, Through the Eyes of... series, Pergamon. Less good than other programmes in the series, but some clips are useful (Key Stages 2–4).

Chapter 5

For the teacher

Tell me a story: story and RE., Maurice Lynch, West London RE Centre. List of
stories for use in RE. (The address is given in Appendix 2.)
The Quest for the Historical Israel, George W Ramsey, SCM Press, 1981.

For the classroom

Key Stage 1
These books are not explicitly religious but raise many of the issues to which
religions provide answers.

Amazing Grace, Mary Hoffman, Frances Lincoln, 1991. The self-image of an
Afro-Caribbean girl who wants to play Peter Pan. The support she receives
and the obstacles she overcomes.
Dinosaurs and all that Rubbish, M Foreman, Hamish Hamilton, 1972. The
dinosaurs return to clear up the mess made by humans. Ecology and
creation related.
Frederick, Leo Lionni, Abelard. Frederick the mouse spends his time musing
on the wonders of the world and neglects to stock his larder against the
arrival of winter.
Frederick's Tales, Leo Lionni, Anderson Press, 1986. Addresses many areas of
human relationships.
Fish is Fish, Leo Lionni, Abelard-Schuman, 1972. A fish discovers the world
beyond his pond from stories told by his friend the frog. An introduction to
the difficult concept of different ways of looking at the world.
John Brown, Rose and the Midnight Cat, Jenny Wagner, Kestrel, 1977. The
effect which a stray cat has on a formerly friendly relationship.
Mama, do you love me?, Barbara Joose, Little, Brown and Company, 1992.
A child tests his mother's love and discovers that she would love
him however dreadful he became, even a monster who frightened her.
Comes as close as anything to the Christian concept of God's forgiving
love.
Nicholas, where have you been?, Leo Lionni, Anderson Press, 1987. A conflict
and hatred story and the solution. Could be frightening.
One World, M Foreman, Anderson Press, 1990. Children make their mini-
world and think about responsibility to the larger world they inhabit.
Tusk Tusk, David McKee, Anderson Press, 1978. A story of hatred between
black and white elephants. Amusing but clear treatment of issues of
prejudice and intolerance.

Key Stage 2

Brother Eagle, Sister Sky, Susan Jeffers, Puffin, 1993. Chief Seattle's view of the world is implicitly contrasted with the typical view of westerners.

Leila, Sue Alexander, Hamish Hamilton, 1988. A Muslim girl helps her father cope with the loss of her brother (also Key Stage 3).

Panda's Puzzle and his Voyage of Discovery, M Foreman, Hamish Hamilton, 1977. Is he a black bear with white bits or a white bear with black bits? Eventually he discovers that he is himself!

Speaking of God, Trevor Dennis, Triangle, 1992. A thought-provoking telling of biblical stories. Plenty to discuss (also Key Stage 3 and upwards).

Tales of the Early World, Ted Hughes, Faber, 1990. Witty accounts of how the world might have come to be.

The Sea People, Jorg Muller and Jorg Steiner, Gollancz, 1982. The story of the contrasting lifestyles and outlooks of the inhabitants of two islands.

The Selfish Giant, Oscar Wilde, Puffin, 1982. An illustrated version of the story about the power of love.

The Whales' Song, Dyan Sheldon and Gary Blythe, Hutchinson, 1988. Grandma and Uncle Frederick tell very different stories about whales. Lily goes down to the jetty to find out for herself.

Chapter 6

For the teacher

An Introduction to the use of Artefacts in RE, Vida Barnett, Articles of Faith.*

Religious Artefacts in the Classroom, P Gateshill and J Thompson, Hodder and Stoughton, 1992.*

For the classroom

Christian Artefacts Pack, Vida Barnett, Articles of Faith.* This takes the form of photocopiable worksheets.

*These and a considerable range of artefacts can be obtained from Articles of Faith. The address is given in Appendix 2.

Chapter 7

For the teacher

Many books on the Bible treat it exclusively as the Christians' book. The teacher who wishes to understand the Jewish context of Christianity and something of their view of the Bible can do no better than read *A History of the Jewish Experience*, L Trepp, Behrmann, 1973.*

Exploring a Theme: Special Books, CEM. Plenty of ideas for primary school teachers.

How to Read the New Testament, E Charpentier, SCM Press, 1981.

How to Read the Old Testament, E Charpentier, SCM Press, 1981.

Introduction to Old Testament Study, J H Hayes, SCM Press, 1992.

People of the Book? The Authority of the Bible in Christianity, J Barton, SPCK, 1978.

The Gospels and Jesus, G Stanton, OUP, 1989.

For the classroom

Book of Bible Stories, Tomie de Paola, Hodder and Stoughton, 1990 (Key Stage 2).

Exploring the Bible, P Curtis, Lutterworth Educational, 1984 (Key Stage 3/4).

The Christian Bible, W Owen Cole, Heinemann Educational, 1993 (Key Stage 3/4).

The Christians' Book, P Curtis, Lutterworth Educational, 1984 (Key Stage 3/4).

The Diary of Anne Frank, Pan, 1953. Still in print and still as powerful (Key Stage 3/4).

This Jewish World, D Charing, Macdonald, 1983 (Key Stage 2/3). A very attractive introduction to Judaism for pupils who know nothing about the religion.*

Video

Message from the Memory Banks, with accompanying booklets, *Considering Origins* and *Considering Meanings*, Janet Green, Bible Society, 1989 (Key Stage 4). One hour, in three twenty-minute parts.

This Land of God. One hour. A tour of the land sacred to three religions (Key Stage 3). *

Windows into Experience, Bible Society, Stonehill Green, Westlea, Swindon SN5 7DG. 90 minutes. Interviews with people for whom the Bible is very important. Costly but can be hired. Long, but can be split into a number of bites (Key Stage 4 and upwards). You could try making your own local version.

(* Can be obtained from Jewish Education Bureau; see Appendix 2.)

Chapter 8

For the teacher

Exploring a Theme: Leaders, CEM. Valuable section on teaching about Jesus for primary school teachers.

For the classroom

Jesus, J F Aylett and R D Holden-Storey, Hodder and Stoughton, 1990 (Key Stage 3/4).

Jesus, T Shannon, Lutterworth, 1982 (Key Stage 3/4).

Jesus and the Birth of the Church, G Windsor and J Hughes, Heinemann Educational, 1990 (Key Stage 3/4).

Jesus World Wide, CEM. Series of six posters of Jesus from different traditions (Key Stage 2 upwards).

Living in the Time of Jesus, P Connolly, OUP, 1983.

The Gospel Story of Jesus, J Thompson, Hodder and Stoughton, 1986 (Key Stage 4/GCSE).

Chapter 9

For the teacher

Contact with local churches is important. They will be able to inform you of hymn books, prayer books and liturgies which they may use, particularly on special occasions, e.g. Good Friday, Easter Day.

Anyone There?, Brenda Lealman, CEM, 1985. Can be used at Key Stage 3 but is likely to be useful to teachers generally.

Investigating Belief in God, K R Chappell, Edward Arnold, 1985 (Key Stage 3/4). Of interest to teachers. Somewhat confessional but emphasizes religious experience.

RE Today, summer 1988, vol 5 no 3. Gives special attention to teaching about God.

For the classroom

Christian Communities, A Brown, Lutterworth Educational, 1982 (Key Stage 3/4).

Christian Experience, C Erricker, Lutterworth Educational, 1982 (Key Stage 3/4).

Christian Worship, J Rankin, Lutterworth Educational, 1982 (Key Stage 3/4).

Colin's Baptism, O Bennett, Hamish Hamilton, 1986 (Key Stage 2).

I am an Anglican, M Killigray, Franklin Watts, 1986 (Key Stage 2).

I am a Greek Orthodox, M Roussou, Franklin Watts, 1985 (Key Stage 2).

I am a Pentacostalist, B Pettenuzzo and C Fairclough, Franklin Watts, 1986 (Key Stage 2).

I am a Roman Catholic, B Pettenuzzo, Franklin Watts, 1986 (Key Stage 2).

Something of a Saint, D M Owen, SPCK, 1990. Lives and prayers of 52 famous Christians in all ages (Key Stage 2/3).

The Pope and the Vatican, R Thomas and J Stutchbury, Macmillan Australia, 1986 (Key Stage 2).

Video

Buildings and Beliefs. English Heritage Education Service, Keysign House, 429 Oxford Street, London W1R 2HD. 20 minutes. Historical. The story of the development of All Saints, York, but can be used in RE if one looks at the purpose and religious function of the building (from Key Stage 3).

Lourdes: Pilgrimage and Healing, St Paul Multimedia Productions, Middle Green, Langley, Slough SL3 6BS. 40 minutes. Can be divided into several sections (Key Stage 4 and upwards).

Chapter 10

For the teacher

Christianity, W Owen Cole, Stanley Thornes, 1989.

Festivals, Family and Food, D Carey and J Large, Hawthorn Press, 1982. Ideas for Key Stage 1/2.

Festivals in World Religions, ed. Alan Brown, Longman, 1994. An academic introduction. (NB The author of the section on Muslim festivals is very dissatisfied with the editing of his essay, which cannot be considered reliable.)

Home, School and Faith, David Rose, David Fulton Publishers, 1992. Extends beyond an examination of festivals but includes them.

The Christian Year, J C J Metford, Thames and Hudson, 1991. A study of the nature and origins of the Christian calendar.

The Christian World, Alan Brown, MacDonald, 1984.

The Way of the Cross from Latin America, Adolfo Esquival, CAFOD. Fourteen pictures of Roman Catholic meditation on Jesus' last journey. Links with ecological concerns, so useful also in Chapters 13 and 15 (Key Stage 3/4).

For the classroom

Easter in Greece, J Vaughan, Macmillan, 1988 (Key Stage 1/2).

Easter in the Orthodox and Western Traditions, a teacher's pack. South London Multifaith RE Centre, Kilmore Road, London SE23. From the same source: *The Orthodox Church*, a teacher's pack.

Religion through Festivals, R O Hughes, Longman, 1989 (Key Stage 2/3).

Video

The Way to Light, St Paul Multimedia Productions. 20 minutes. A meditation on the passion and resurrection of Jesus, based on the art of Marcello Silvestri. Could help older pupils reflect on the meaning of Easter for Christians (Key Stage 4 and upwards).

Chapter 11

For the teacher

Books listed in the general Bibliography and Chapter 10, plus:

Celebrating Christmas, CEM, 1986.
Christmas, A Ewans, RMEP, 1982.

For the classroom

'Christmas 5–14', *Teaching RE*, Autumn 1992.
My Class at Christmas, Watts, 1986, (Key Stage 1/2).
The Nativity, Julie Vivas, Cambridge University Press, 1982 (Key Stage 1).
   Teachers will need to adapt the words from this King James Version text
   but the illustrations are excellent. Likewise:
Christmas, Jan Pienkowski, Heinemann, 1984.
'Christmas around the world', *Child Education*, December 1992, Scholastic
   Publications (Key Stage 2/3).
Gifts and the gift-bringers, Judith Lowndes, the Exploring a Theme series, CEM.

Chapter 12

For the teacher

A Report on Afro-Caribbean Christianity in Britain, V Howard, University of
   Leeds Dept of Religious Studies, 1987.
The Orthodox Church, Timothy Ware, Mowbray, 1967.
The Orthodox Church, Timothy Ware, Penguin, 1963.

For the classroom

An Ebony Cross, I Smith and and W Green, Marshall Pickering, 1989.
   Contains case study material useful at Key Stage 3/4.
Living in Harmony – The Story of Sybil Phoenix, John Newbury, RMEP, 1985.
   Mrs Phoenix is a well-known British black Christian (Key Stage 2/3).
Medieval Islam, P Bartley and H Bourdillon, Hodder and Stoughton, 1993.
The Crusades, P Mantin and R Pulley, Hodder and Stoughton, 1993 (Key
   Stage 3/4).
The Islamic World, P Mantin and R Mantin, CUP, 1993.

Teachers including the Holocaust or Crusades in RE might use the following:
Dying We Live, eds. H Gollwitzer, K Kuhn and R Schneider, Harvill Press,
   1956. The last letters or observers' memories of executed opponents of
   Hitler, ranging from a farm boy to aristocrats and theologians (Key Stage 3
   selectively, Key Stage 4 and upwards).

Smoke and Ashes, OUP, 1991 (Key Stage 3). A study of the Holocaust for slightly older pupils.*

The Number on my Grandfather's Arm, 1987 (Key Stage 2). A moving story which will help children understand the Holocaust.*

Video

Dear Kitty. 27 minutes. Children witness the Holocaust (Key Stage 2).*

ITV Believe it or Not series, CV0141, CV0142, CV0143, CV0144, Articles of Faith. Each video contains several programmes, not all on Christianity. Subjects include confirmation, Salvation Army, Caribbean Roman Catholic and Pentecostal (Key Stage 2/3).

The Black Pentecostal Experience, ILEA. Available from Educational Media, 235 Imperial Drive, Rayners Lane, Harrow, Middlesex HA2 7HE.

The Holocaust and Yad Vashem, 30 minutes. Takes the viewer through the sequence of events which led to the Holocaust and then into its course (Key Stage 4 and upwards).

(*Can be obtained from the Jewish Education Bureau; see Appendix 2.)

Chapter 13

For the teacher

Christian Ethics in a Secular World, R Gill, Clark, 1991.

Exploring a Theme: the Environment, CEM. Good ideas for teaching about environmental issues in the primary school.

Groundwork of Christian Ethics, R G Jones, Epworth, 1984.

For the classroom

Contemporary Moral Issues, J Jenkins, Heinemann Educational, 1989 and 1992.

Ethics and Religions, J Rankin, A Brown and P Gateshill, Longman, 1991.

Introducing Moral Issues, J Jenkins, Heinemann Educational, 1994.

Moral Issues in Six Religions, ed. W Owen Cole, Heinemann Educational, 1991.

Chapter 14

For the teacher

General

The Quiet Revolution, R Banks, Lion, 1985 and 1989.

Inter-religious encounter

All their Splendours, David Brown, Fount, 1982.

The Bible and People of Other Faiths, W Ariarajah, World Council of Churches, 1985.

What is Idolatry?, Roger Hooker, The British Council of Churches, 1986. Hooker was a CMS missionary for many years, during which time he also studied Hinduism and Sanskrit. The book is available from the bookshop at Inter-Church House, 35–41 Lower Marsh, London SE1 7RL.

Liberation theology

The Christian World, Alan Brown, MacDonald, 1984.
Images of Jesus, A Wessels, SCM Press, 1990.
Introducing Liberation Theology, C and L Boff, Burns and Oates, 1987.
Theology and Politics, D B Forester, Blackwell, 1988.
Voices from the Margin – Interpreting the Bible in the Third World, ed. R S Sugirtharajah, SPCK, 1991.

Women in Christianity

Feminist Interpretation of the Bible, ed. L Russell, Blackwell, 1986.
Feminist Theology, A Reader, ed. A Loades, SPCK, 1990.
Herstory: Women in the Christian Tradition, B MacHaffie, Fortress, 1986.
The Divine Feminine: The Biblical Imagery of God as Female, V R Mollencott, Crossroads, 1983.
Womanspirit Rising – A Feminist Reader in Religion, C Christ and J Plaskow, Harper, 1979.
Women and Spirituality, U King, Macmillan, 1989.

For the classroom

Being a Christian, A Wood, BFSS National RE Centre (address in Appendix 2), 1990. The personal beliefs of a number of Christians from different backgrounds (Key Stage 3/4).
Christianity, a Living Faith, B Wintersgill, Macmillan, 1989 (Key Stage 4). Presents Christianity as a broad and diverse religion.

Chapter 16

For the teacher

Teaching World Religions, ed. Clive Erricker, Heinemann Educational, 1993.

For the classroom

Christianity and Homosexuality, Lesbian and Gay Christian Movement, Oxford House, Derbyshire Street, London E2 6HG, 1992. A resource for students which may be used from Key Stage 4 and perhaps in a course of ethics, but more likely in sixth form studies.

Video

Humanism, the Great Detective Story, The British Humanist Association, Lamb's Conduit Passage, London WC1R 4RH. 21 minutes (also at Key Stage 4).

Index